# Foul Deeds and Suspicious Deaths in Grimsby and Cleethorpes

# Foul Deeds & Suspicious Deaths in

# GRIMSBY & CLEETHORPES

## Stephen Wade

*Series Editor*
**Brian Elliott**

**Wharncliffe Books**

First published in Great Britain in 2007 by
Wharncliffe Local History
*an imprint of*
Pen & Sword Books Ltd
47 Church Street
Barnsley
South Yorkshire
S70 2AS

ISBN 978 1 84563 027 0

Typeset in Plantin and Benguiat by
Phoenix Typesetting, Auldgirth, Dumfriesshire

Printed and bound in England by
CPI UK

Pen & Sword Books Ltd incorporates the imprints of Pen
& Sword Aviation, Pen & Sword Maritime,
Pen & Sword Military, Wharncliffe Local History, Pen
and Sword Select, Pen and Sword Military Classics and
Leo Cooper.


For a complete list of Pen & Sword titles please contact
PEN & SWORD BOOKS LIMITED
47 Church Street
Barnsley
South Yorkshire
S70 2AS, England
E-mail: enquiries@pen-and-sword.co.uk
Website: www.pen-and-sword.co.uk

# Contents

Acknowledgements      vii

Introduction      1

Chapter 1    Havelok the Dane      4

Chapter 2    Smugglers' Tales Through the Centuries      7

Chapter 3    Barons and Bailiffs in the Middle Ages      12

Chapter 4    Grimsby Men Take on Henry VIII      15

Chapter 5    Crime in the Countryside during the 1830s      19

Chapter 6    Fatal Stabbing at the *Duke of York*, 1831      26

Chapter 7    Violence at the Elections, 1862 and 1877      31

Chapter 8    Problems for the New Police, 1850–1900      35

Chapter 9    Neglect on a Train, 1860      39

Chapter 10    Rape on the Dock, 1866      42

Chapter 11    Brutal Murder of a Wife, 1887      45

Chapter 12    Hard Labour for Oyster Stealing, 1887      50

Chapter 13    Cigars in the Death Cell, 1893      53

Chapter 14    Fraud and Cruelty: Extreme Crimes at the Century's End      57

Chapter 15    Apprentices, Hard Times and Lincoln Gaol, 1850–1900      61

Chapter 16    Tough Lives for Child Slaves, c.1900      66

Chapter 17    Lock-Out Trouble, 1901      71

Chapter 18    A Murdering Mariner, 1903      76

Chapter 19    Capture of a Spy, 1915      79

Chapter 20    Cruelty to an Objector, Cleethorpes, 1917      83

Chapter 21    Poor Law Guardian Murdered, 1919      86

| | | |
|---|---|---|
| **Chapter 22** | Cruelty in the Village, 1919 | **91** |
| **Chapter 23** | The Jockey Con Man, 1919 | **94** |
| **Chapter 24** | Wages Gone Astray, 1922 | **96** |
| **Chapter 25** | Car Crime Wave, 1937 | **99** |
| **Chapter 26** | The Story of *The Girl Pat* Libel, 1937–38 | **103** |
| **Chapter 27** | Brawls and Incidents for the New Constable, 1930s | **107** |
| **Chapter 28** | A Fuss Over a Thief's Appeal, 1949 | **113** |
| **Chapter 29** | Robbery With Violence, 1953 | **115** |
| **Chapter 30** | Indecency at the Seaside? 1954 | **121** |
| **Chapter 31** | Seaman on a Crime Spree, 1954 | **126** |
| **Chapter 32** | Bravery at Gunpoint, 1955 | **130** |
| **Chapter 33** | A Vagrancy Issue, 1955 | **134** |
| **Chapter 34** | Double Murder, 1959 | **137** |
| **Chapter 35** | A Sad Case, 1959 | **143** |
| **Chapter 36** | The Pirate Trawlermen, 1966 | **147** |
| **Chapter 37** | Why Was He Set Free? 1967 | **150** |
| **Chapter 38** | Some Curiosities Not So Foul | **153** |
| **Bibliography and Sources** | | **162** |
| **Index** | | **165** |

# Acknowledgements

Thanks go to various people and organisations who have helped with materials and illustrations: Louise Hickman; library staff in Grimsby, *The Evening Telegraph* and many local enthusiasts. The writings of those talented historians Rex Russell and B J Davey have been particularly useful. For the truly human element in crime, I have to thank Bert Fryer for his memoir of life as a police constable in the 1930s and 1940s. Further appreciation is also due to Grimsby Library for permission to use material from the Skelton Collection. The posters from the 1830s reproduced here are from the Skelton.

There have also been documents from people who remain anonymous, such as the police officer who owned my copy of the Lincolnshire Constabulary Instruction Book for 1920. His manuscript notes proved to be a delight and an historian's dream.

I must also thank Ros Boyce at Lincolnshire Archives and Ann Tate and Garry Crosland at the Port of Grimsby for their help with the Donald McGill story and with their efforts to educate me about the docks as they would have been back in the high summer of Grimsby's boom years as a fishing town.

The prints of police officers and of Superintendent George Stennett are by permission of the Local Studies Collection, Lincoln Central Library. The images of the fishing smack and of the trawlers during the strike are by permission of The Museum of Lincolnshire Life, both by courtesy of Lincolnshire County Council.

Finally, thanks also to Paul Williams of *Murder Files* for help with research.

# Introduction

Regional crime in Britain tends to make readers think of very highly populated places, usually with heavy industry and massive immigration. We expect violent crime to reflect social conflicts and these are easily located in the Industrial Revolution. But some towns, in many ways on the periphery even in Victorian years, have their share of 'foul deeds' and in many ways these stories have a special interest for us, as they reflect societies which had problems of their own, off the track, as it were. In some ways, this describes the town of Grimsby.

For the poets, the Humber estuary is 'the end of England' as Philip Larkin put it. There is a sense in which that long sky-line and the North Sea beyond makes the panorama both monotonous but also beautiful. Earlier writers have not been complimentary. In 1926, W F Rawnsley said: 'This [Grimsby] is not at all an imposing or handsome town, but the length of the timber docks, the pontoons which project into the river and are crowded with fishing boats . . . are a wonderful sight.' There is much more history to this part of the Humber estuary than meets the eye. We have to work harder and ask more questions to find the hidden history and the human stories.

In the eighteenth century, the writer and author of *Robinson Crusoe*, Daniel Defoe, came to the town and his verdict was: 'Grimsby is a good town, but I think 'tis but an indifferent road for shipping; and in the great storm (1703) it was proved to be so, for almost all the ships that lay in Grimsby road were driven from their anchors and many of them lost . . .' Things of that nature were sorted out after Defoe's time.

In terms of law and crime, the police force was formed in 1846 and became part of Lincolnshire in 1967. It began with just four officers, and had 237 at its demise. When the town was a really great port, the chief constables had a particularly massive task. In 1930, arguably, Grimsby was the greatest fishing port in the world. There were 500 trawlers based there. Timber was also a large part of the commerce at the time, being at the end of the chain of communication north of the Trent navigation. The town's population had boomed between the last years of the Victorian period to the 1930s, growing from around 40,000 in

1880 to 90,000 by 1930. The 1930s were a very unusual period in the town's criminal history: John Wilson estimates that there were no murders between 1930 and 1936, and that there were only about fifty assaults in each of those years. The memoirs of Bert Fryer (see bibliography) confirm this, with a rather comic and easy-going memoir of the police work there at the time, involving drunks and humorous antics.

Many of the problems came from outsiders, in fact, as Frank L Bun records in his book, *No Silver Spoon*: 'One of the first duties falling to my lot in Grimsby was the very necessary elimination of a number of unscrupulous persons who were imposing on the public outside the town, and who, by their fraudulent behaviour, were likely to bring honest fish merchants into disrepute.'

The nineteenth century was very different. Many of the cases recalled here concern assaults, drunken violence, rick-burning and animal theft or maiming; the century takes the historian from political violence and rural confrontation to transportation and then to social disorder. As with every other thriving Victorian town, along with the progress came the poverty, the gap in wealth and the communal violence.

When the Humber made the news in past years, it was often with the sea in mind, naturally, and the case studies in this book often relate to the ships, the fishing fleets and even pirates. Not only was there great power in the hands of a skipper of a fishing vessel: there was also the hierarchy of command and an apprentice system. This meant the potential for abuses of that power. Perhaps the most sensational story in that context comes from Hull: the murderous cruelty of Otto Brand, eventually hanged for his killing of a fisher boy. But Grimsby has its tales as well.

Of course, in the early years of the nineteenth century, many 'crimes' at the time strike us now as being totally understandable – acts done in desperation, poverty and starvation. But the punishments were brutal. There were over 200 capital crimes on the statute book until the reforms of the 1830s when Sir Robert Peel's penal and police acts began to have an impact. For instance, David Stattersfield of Grimsby was sentenced to seven years' transportation in 1829; he was just twenty years old and had perpetrated a minor theft (by modern standards). Three labourers from Louth for 'unlawfully entering a parcel of land' were given three months in prison.

But there are also stories here from much earlier in history. We have to start with the tale of *Havelok the Dane*, written in the thirteenth century. This is the story of a dispossessed prince, brought up in Grimsby by Grim, a man who eventually struggles to win back his crown. The Seal of Grimsby relates to this, dating from the reign of Edward I (1272–1307) and showing three characters: Grim, Havelock and Goldborough – and a ray of light, hinting at the high destiny of our hero.

There is also the part played by Grimsby and the surrounding areas in the massive events of the Pilgrimage of Grace of 1536. Once again, an example of legal and illegal confrontations that present the modern reader with 'crimes' that will be hard to define in terms outside the Tudor view of the world.

Overall, though, the stories here are about ordinary men and women, living routine lives, but their tales are often of their being pushed too far or making a terribly bad decision; giving in to violence when drunk, or letting jealousy and hatred dominate them. The people of the past were very much like us, but we have to dig under the surface to understand what stresses and strains they were subject to. Looking at the history of crime is a unique way to see and understand these communal forces and personal impulses.

The Grimsby area has always reared hardy, tough characters with spirit and a sense of adventure. Two such men were Tom Wintringham and Edward Dickinson. The first was born in Grimsby in 1898, the son of the town's most successful maritime lawyer. The second was born in 1903 and both were to fight in the Spanish Civil War. Tom became a poet. Edward, the son of a fish merchant, was active in politics in Australia and had he stayed in Grimsby he may have figured in a chapter in this book because he fought a duel with Italy's foreign minister over the Italian invasion of Abyssinia (now Ethiopia). Edward was shot by the Fascists in Spain. Memoirs refer to him as a 'born leader'. Maybe Grimsby creates personalities who have the trawler skipper attitude, and Edward Dickinson showed that, for sure.

These stories recall more than mere crimes. They are about controversies, bad choices and social upheaval, class conflict and abuse of power. Many stories, like some of the fish, 'got away' such as the full story of William Hall of Grimsby, who stabbed Edward Button in the neck. Hall was just twenty-two and was hanged at Lincoln.

# CHAPTER 1

# Havelok the Dane

## The myth is a tale wrapped in storms, pirates and fights to right a wrong . . .

E very place likes to have an exciting story attached to it and Grimsby is no exception.

Whether there is any truth in the great foundation story of Grimsby we will never know, but one thing is for sure: the stories of how Havelok set Grimsby on its path through history is a compelling narrative – a myth wrapped in storms, pirates and fights to right a wrong. Havelok's tale is one of the very oldest in English literature. Experts think it was written around the year 1300 and shreds of it still exist in the famous Havelok Stone located outside the current Grimsby Institute of Further and Higher Education.

The tale starts in England with the death of King Athelwold, who left no son to take over his power. The Earl of Cornwall was in charge until the king's daughter, Goldborow, was old enough to marry and she was to be destined to marry the top man around in Britain at the time. But when the king died, Cornwall had the girl locked away.

In Denmark, another king died and another man was made Regent until the son, Havelok, was old enough to take power. The Regent was the first in a line of horrible murderers in the tale, and he gave little Havelok to Grim, a fisherman, to be drowned. But from that point the destiny of Grimsby is foretold, as the fisherman saw that the boy was special. The myth says that he had a bright light shining from his mouth – something called a 'kynemark'. This is the point at which Grim and Havelok run away and make landfall in Lincolnshire.

The first nasty business in the tale takes place in the North Sea on the way to Grimsby, as pirates attack them. Everyone is massacred except for Grim and Havelok. So they settle in Grimsby and Grim brought Havelok up well and the boy became strong and well-built. He is a real success, but his father reckoned

THE

# MONUMENTAL ANTIQUITIES

OF

## GREAT GRIMSBY.

### AN ESSAY

TOWARDS ASCERTAINING ITS ORIGIN AND

## ANCIENT POPULATION.

CONTAINING ALSO

A BRIEF ACCOUNT OF THE TWO MAGNIFICENT CHURCHES AND THE FIVE
RELIGIOUS HOUSES, WHICH WERE ONCE THE GRACE AND ORNA-
MENT OF THE TOWN; AN ABSTRACT OF THE CHARTERS
AND PRIVILEGES OF THE BOROUGH; BIOGRAPHICAL
NOTICES OF EMINENT NATIVES OF GRIMSBY;
LISTS OF HIGH STEWARDS, MEMBERS
OF PARLIAMENT, &c.

*The whole collected from original and authentic Sources.*

### BY GEORGE OLIVER,

VICAR OF CLEE,

DOMESTIC CHAPLAIN TO THE RIGHT HONOURABLE LORD KENSINGTON, AUTHOR OF
"THE ANTIQUITIES OF FREE MASONRY," &c.

### HULL:

PRINTED BY ISAAC WILSON, LOWGATE.

1825.

Title page of one of the early histories of Grimsby, with the Havelok tale
prominent. Author's collection

that the boy needed to go away somewhere more sophisticated and learn more about life. Havelok went to Lincoln and there he did well, catching the eye of the powerful Godrich (Cornwall) who marries the lad to Goldborow. Marrying a strong but penniless young man seemed to be the best way to keep her away from anything that might be called a rising career. But they run away back to Grimsby and there the prophecy is told to Goldborow that she has in fact married a man who should be king.

Havelok has a hard time in Lincoln, though, being someone who made enemies, but one writer says that Havelok had a dark side, and that if he was set against one of his enemies he would tie him up. In fact, he is something of a villain in the story as well, because he was not averse to doing some nasty work. As the historian Edward Gillett has noted: 'Havelok is enough of a Christian to vow that he will found a house of black monks but still enough of a pagan to burn churches and strangle monks and nuns.' We have to conclude that in those days winning was not something that the virtuous could accomplish by simply being good. They had also to be as ruthless as their enemies and, after all, the man had to take a huge area of land from Lincoln to the Humber, as he was confronting a man who ruled from Lincoln.

The different versions of the tale make the fights and confrontations rather different, but he has to fight for his throne. When Godard is beaten, Havelok has to come home and fight for his land and his dominion. All in all, this was a story to start the saga of Grimsby off on a footing of hatred, divided families and revenge. But for the story of crime in the place, we have to say that the real villains of the piece were the pirates. No doubt they were from the Humber and found anyone daring to travel all the way from Denmark to Grimsby to be easy prey.

Somewhere underneath all the folklore there are traces of real history, but whatever the truth about Grim and Havelok, the story sets the tone for many later 'ripping yarns' that come along with the often desperate accounts of real crime.

This could have easily never happened at all – Havelok, when very young, was faced with a threat of murder and Grim had to protect him through his growing-up, knowing that the boy had enemies. The Seal of Grimsby shows us an image of Grim, very warlike, no doubt warding off villains, so somehow it sets the tone for some of the dark tales to come in Grimsby's criminal history.

# CHAPTER 2

# Smugglers' Tales Through the Centuries

## The poor devil called the Riding Officer was always a victim

I n 1690, down in Romney Marsh, the post of Riding Officer was established. This meant that a man in uniform was to ride on patrol, covering several miles of coast, looking out for smugglers and contraband goods, i.e. vessels off shore and nefarious activities by moonlight. Of course, smuggling was a standard version of a local economy through the centuries but something had to be done and that was just one of many measures taken that did not work very well. The unfortunate Riding Officer was always a victim. On the east coast of Yorkshire on one occasion one such officer had not been paid for three months and had to write to his master begging for his wages.

This by-way of local history is one that existed alongside smuggling – a major business enterprise for a very long period. The shores of the Humber and the narrow river courses of North Lincolnshire were perfect smuggler territory. In the seventeenth and eighteenth centuries it was rife. In the 1700s there was a large excise duty on such luxuries as tea and tobacco so a black market inevitably grew. But there are case studies from much earlier, such as that of William de Len and his gang from Louth who, in the thirteenth century, sold 200 sacks of wool to merchants over the North Sea, taking them over the sea with the aid of bribes.

In the ancient records of the Court of Star Chamber, a court that in Tudor times was to restrain 'over mighty subjects' and dealt with everything from sedition to top-class theft and assault, there are accounts of Humber pirates and remarkably one documented story of these villains links to the Abbot of Whitby. The Abbot in the late sixteenth century had dealings with a gang

Old print showing the excise man being duped by a smuggler. Author's collection

described by one early writer as doing 'questionable trans-actions'. Little more is known about some mysterious crooks called Ganth, Lappage and Parys, but in a 'ring' with the Abbot and with a powerful local magnate called Conyers, they plied their trade.

Ganth was arraigned for carrying, among other goods, some-thing called 'osmonds' and the antiquarian Edward Peacock suggests that these were 'the very best iron used for the finest purposes such as arrow-heads, fish-hooks, the repairs of bell-gear and the works of clocks'. Ganth was going to get very rich on this trade in osmonds along the Humber, after docking in the Humber his French colleagues shipped materials up the coast to the Abbot. It was all very lucrative, until the Star Chamber men found out. There is no record of what the punishment was, but we know that the officers of the Chamber put pressure on jurors to ignore the truth and find guilt where the desire to convict was strong. The Tudor monarchs hated the thought of any other faction or group having any degree of power that might be too grand, and smuggling was a way to have that status.

Smuggling and piracy were often so large-scale an enterprise

# EXECUTIONS.

1806  Thomas Temporal, alias Otter, for the mur of Mary Kirkham, whom ' had wedded on the same day as he committed the foul deed, and having at the same time a wife and child at a village near Southwell. He confessed his guilt. His body was, after execution, taken from the Castle to Saxilby Moor, and hung in chains, near the very place where the horrid deed was done. Also hung at the same time D. Dickenson and T. Kirton, for sheep stealing

1813  G. T. Rowell, A. Fountain, murder, D. Spreadbury, forgery

1814  W. Ward, for burglary, and last executed on the old gallows

1815  Thomas Clarke and Henry Coster, for burglary.

1816  March 15th—Eliz. Whiting, for murder. This was the first person executed on the new drop. July 16th—Eliz. Warrener for murder. Aug. 15th—W. Longland, for burglary

1818  March 27th—Richard Randall and John Tubs, for highway robbery ; Thos. Morris and Thos. Evison, for firing

1819  March 19—Louth, burglary ; Aug. 16, Johnson horse stealing

1821  March 23rd—David Booth and John Parish, for house breaking. Aug. 9th—James Cawthorne for murder

1822  March 22nd—Rogers, for robbery ; Aug. 2, Burkitt, robbery

1823  March 21st—B. Candler, W. Arden, and J. Doughty, for rape

1824  March 14—J. Smith, murder ; Aug. 20—J. Wetherill, murder

1827  March 23rd—William Udale, for sheep stealing

1829  March 27th—T. Lister, for burglary ; G. Wingfield, for highway robbery. The last man that was hung at the city prison

1830  March 19th—T. Strong and T. Brammar (alias Tiger Tom) for housebreaking. John Clarke, for sheep stealing.

1831  March 12th—Michael Lundy for murder ; 18th—John Greenwood, for burglary ; July 22nd—William Hall for murder ; 29th—Richard Cooling & Thomas Motley for firing

1833  March 18th—W. Taylor, for murder ; 22nd—W. Stephenson for highway robbery ; July 26th—T. Knapton, for rape

1843  March 17th—Thomas Johnson, for murder

1844  Aug. 2nd—Eliza Joyce, for murder, at Boston

1847  July 30th—Mary Ann Milner, under sentence of death for murder by poisoning, was found dead in her cell on the morning of her execution, she having hung herself with a silk handkerchief. Culprits were never left alone again.

1849  July 27th—John Ward for the murder of his mother. He ascended the scaffold 2 steps at once. Calcraft executed.

1859  Aug. 5th—William Pickett and Henry Carey, for the murder of William Stephenson, of Sibsey, near Boston. The day of their execution was fine, and the crowd of people was estimated to be about 25,000. Askern was the executioner

1868  Dec. 28th—Priscilla Biggadyke, for the murder of her husband by poisoning, on the 1st October. This wretched murderess was the first that was hung under the Private Executions' Act, which was strictly adhered to, the officials of the prison and four reporters being the only persons present, besides the chaplin, under-sheriff, and Askern, the executioner. She protested her innocence to the last.

1872  April 1st—Wm. Fredk. Horry, 28, for the murder of his wife Jane Horry, by shooting her, at Boston. Great interest was taken in this culprit's case, and the following were his last words on the scaffold :—The Chaplain: " God bless you, are you thoroughly resigned and do you die in full reliance of the forgiveness

List of executions at Lincoln Castle, 1880. From Ward's *Historical Guide to Lincoln*. Author's collection

that the authorities could do nothing. In the early sixteenth century there were so many Scottish ships in the Humber estuary that local captains were afraid to set out to sea; there would be a ransom to be paid if they did. There were also local squabbles such as that two merchants fell out and one slandered the other by saying that the 'false wretch' had hidden away sheep skins and not paid duty on them. Many men were found out, of course. One historian recorded a number of offenders who had been breaking the law on a grand scale:

> . . . it was ascertained by a jury, impanelled for the purpose, that Roger de Brigsley had shipped six sacks of wool, of the value of seven marks per sack, at the port of Grimsby for export into Flanders . . . and that William Sevenac at the same time sent five sacks of wool in sheets, price eight marks each . . . and at Easter he smuggled five sacks more..

Even with the arrival of an efficient coastal excise patrol in the nineteenth century, smugglers abounded, such as Thomas Lumley who was fined the massive sum of £1,500 in 1826. Lumley would store his goods in a barn at Stallingborough and then take them to Aylesby Church where he would use the tower to detain them. It has been suggested that the name New Holland was created from this trade in illicit gin because the old name for gin was 'Hollands gin' or, in Dutch, *Hollandsch genever*.

In 1869, a gang comprising George Atkinson, Stephen Andrews, Edwin Bray and Palmer Bray were charged with smuggling. The accused were all firemen on the steamship, *Grimsby*. A customs officer called Mumby boarded the ship before she left for Hamburg. When he went into the engine-room he found sixty packages of tobacco in a waste-locker. It was his second search of the vessel and maybe at that point he would have been satisfied that the men were just working on a moderate level of petty crime.

But the tobacco had been kept in some waterproof tin cases so Mumby's suspicions were aroused that such storage methods would not prevent further underwater contraband being around the ship. Consequently, he pumped under the boiler and there he found a space of two feet between the boiler and the framework of the ship; only by going under the boiler could the goods have been taken out, and there was more.

The culprits were given a heavy fine of £100 and that they would be kept in Lincoln Castle prison until the fines were paid. That was a huge sum of money then, and the papers reported, some weeks after, that the fines were not paid. Mumby had done some detective work and spotted that some trousers and a Guernsey sweater had had tobacco packed in them and stuffed under the boiler as well.

Such cases were common and it has to be said that the common view was the risks were worth the potential profits. Mumby's occupation was a lot more secure and prestigious than his predecessor, the poor riding officer.

# CHAPTER 3

# Barons and Bailiffs in the Middle Ages

## There were private injuries and open quarrels

n 1255 King Henry III was taking on the powerful barons of the kingdom, trying to wrest back some authority. It became a matter of economic influence and as always in these things, the other poor folk in the kingdom suffer as the repercussions affect the lower classes of society. The great landmark of the Magna Carta, in 1215, was within living memory of many at the time, and the King issued patents to the local power-base, so along came the choking monopolies of trade.

In Grimsby, the fishermen reached the point at which they had to trade abroad rather than in their home town. One earlier writer notes that: 'The town of Grimsby became a theatre of strife and the lower class of its inhabitants accused the opulent burgesses of a lawless and violent usurpation of their liberties.' What had to happen was that the central forces of law had to act. The inevitable followed. Gilbert de Preston arrived with the brief of making a report of what was going on.

The aristocrats and wealthy merchants were holding ships at sea or in harbour and then buying the cargoes very cheaply. They could then resell at an immense profit and the poor traders were being squeezed out. Of course, this was illegal – it was technically 'forestalling' but this time, unusual in criminal history, the rich were acting like pirates. Gilbert could understand this, but could do nothing to stop a local civil war situation. Some of the stronger and less malleable characters took on William de Waltham and his pals. First, one Simon de Watchet grabbed Holm Manor and blocked the roads. He strung an iron chain across the Weelby road and charged a toll. Then, as sides were taken and allies asked to help, things came to an extreme impasse as the bailiff of the Earl of Lincoln told his servants to seize a horse and cart belonging to a town burgess. Amazingly, he managed to imprison this man with his family, in a gaol at Waltham and they could only be freed when ten marks was paid to Roger. He made a habit of this, and his servants were becoming no more than a criminal gang. Alan de Kyrketon was brave enough to take them on but he paid the price, being severely beaten up and left mortally wounded.

The fight accelerated when Walter de la Lindes of Little Cotes took hold of the port of Friskney. When people stood up to him they were locked up at Laceby. His men stole goods, refused to pay taxes and generally ran the show in a place where there should have been free trade and open commerce to all towns-people in a chartered borough. What was happening was anarchy, something that the whole state had known before in several reigns, and notably in the years of Stephen and Matilda a century earlier. Even the religious principals were subject to these aggressive constraints on land and roads. The Abbot of Wellow blocked a road and the Knights Templars, who were powerful feudal magnates in the town, dammed a stream and cut off fresh water for ordinary folk.

Crown property had been taken by force, and by private individuals. Something had to be done, and before a new corporation charter could be given, a bailiffs' court was instituted to try to set things right. Any further escalation of these open quarrels and abuses would have led to violence and murder. In 1259, an investigation led to a provision that merchants had to sell their goods within markets established by tradition and common goodwill. It was meant to protect the civil liberties of the weaker or less wealthy town burgesses. Through all these terrible events there were private injuries and open quarrels, as one writer has put it. That is a way of explaining the kind of resentment and aggression that leads to the worst kind of civil unrest and riot.

These kinds of violent and brutal events, happening with a background in which the powerful customarily took by force what they wanted, reminds us today that in the centuries before an established police force, the general pattern of legal and moral obligations could easily slip into the anarchy of clannish vendetta and a 'might is right' frame of mind. One effect of all this was that the Knights Templars in the town were dissolved soon after this turbulent period. It is a mark of the power of the burgesses and landed aristocrats such as the de Lindes that this could be achieved.

In the end, these troubles had to stop before they moved into much broader arenas of commercial allegiances and drew in factions from afar. It was a close-run affair and many must have feared the worst.

# CHAPTER 4

# Grimsby Men Take on Henry VIII

## Robert Constable inherited his relish for a fight from his headstrong father . . .

I n 1536, there were many parts of the north of Henry VIII's realm in which men were discontented and it was growing worse. What the king and his advisers didn't realise for some time was that among the restless men were some powerful ones. It was going to be a tough year for thousands of people in England. Some of those malcontents were in North Lincolnshire and that area was to be one of the focal points of dissent. The words of a Victorian writer explain the depth of the feeling towards their sovereign: 'The driving forth of monks, many old and infirm, and of timid nuns, into the wide world of which they knew nothing, shocked the sensibilities of the lower orders, who could sympathise with distress, and who, opening their hovels to receive the outcasts, gathered from their recital of indignities exasperation against the government which did these wrongs.'

The richer folk would also suffer but in different ways. If abbots were thrown out of their positions, then the wealthy would lose a person who had been, as Robert Aske was to say 'who had been the trustees of their children and the executors of their wills . . .'

What happened as a result of this militancy has been called the Pilgrimage of Grace and it was the most bitter and troublesome uprising of several such stirrings in Henry's land. The fundamental cause was in the dissolution of the monasteries, but that effort to increase the royal revenue was just one of many such fund-raising exploits that angered the ordinary folk. When a royal commission arrived in Louth the discontent transmuted into rebellion and the Lincolnshire Rising began. Paradoxically, the rebellion as a whole was led by a Yorkshireman, Robert Aske. He had land just across the Humber and so North Lincolnshire and the Louth and Grimsby areas were not so far away.

Estimates about the numbers of men in the north who rallied to the cause are around 30,000. It has to be remembered that there was no national military structure in place and the sovereigns had to rely on aristocrats in the regions to respond to a call to arms in cases like this. The Dukes of Norfolk and Suffolk had the command to meet the rebels but it was soon realised that armed confrontation was likely to fail. Henry had other weapons to use and some of these were mere words.

What was really hurting the people was the taxation imposed on them and the petty strictures, laws and ordinances levelled against everyday activity. The phrase of modern times, 'police state' is not far from the truth. In Lincolnshire the leader who emerged at the time was Nicholas Melton from Louth, a shoe-maker. Melton acquired a nickname – Captain Cobbler – and he began to plan militant action against a government that was perceived as heartless, distant and uncaring. Henry had disposed of vast tracts of monastic lands and he had increased both direct and indirect taxes to breaking point. Northerners felt very far away from places where government happened and laws were made – and not simply in geographical terms. Grudges increased as men were executed for relatively minor offences. The last straw for Lincolnshire men was the punishment of a local man, a vicar of Louth, Thomas Kendall. His basic beliefs were under trial in this new regime of Henry's and he did what he did best in his profession: he gave a sermon which was easily interpreted as a spur to the locals to rebel against tyranny.

The church bells were rung backwards – a sign that there was trouble on the way in Lincolnshire. Into this atmosphere of serious unrest came the figure of Guy Kyme and he became the key link-man between Aske's Yorkshire men and the Lincolnshire rebels. In no time, a force of over 3,000 men were on the march from Louth to Caistor. In Grimsby there was much support and from there came the charismatic Sir Robert Constable, who inherited his relish for a fight from his head-strong father, Thomas Constable of Great Grimsby. Thomas was born in Nuneaton around 1506. He married Barbara Catherall and they had two children, Robert and Ursula. Thomas found himself in a fight with some of Sir William Percy's men, as there was a feud going on between the families.

Robert was soon involved in the coming trouble against Henry and it was destined to be a tragic tale. It appears that the rebels actually gathered their guns in Grimsby. A number of well-known Grimsby men joined the rebels and Constable was not the only active leader. William Morland also came to the town under the pretence of bringing official religious papers, but his real purpose in being there, as the government officials later thought, was to incite rebellion. Guy Kyme also came to the town with the same objective. Support was strong, as in the case of Richard Thimolby and his brother John who gathered a small army. There was also Anthony Curtis from Clee, who was favourable to the cause. This was all going on early in the year and it would be near the end of the year before any crown forces or ships arrived in Grimsby. Over those seven months, a great deal of activity among the rebel forces went on, including the murder of one of the Lord Burgh's servants near Caistor.

Of all the men involved in the rising who spent time in the town, Kyme was the one who was almost certainly on the most important and large-scale assignment, potentially working to link the northern shores of the Humber and men as far as Scarborough with the North Lincolnshire groups. But the organisation in Lincolnshire was not as efficient and well-led as in Yorkshire. Much of the criticism levelled against the Lincolnshire rebels came from such Victorian writers as Sabine-Gould, who described them as '. . . assembling and marching in unwieldy crowds, without chiefs or discipline, accoutrements or provisions . . .' But the fact is that the central character in the whole northern rebellion, Robert Aske, was crossing the Humber from his land in Ellerker to Barton and the area between Louth and Immingham, trying to bring in some real integration in the different areas; church bells had been rung and beacons lit. There were genuine attempts to sue the time-honoured methods of communicating rebellious intensions.

Guy Kyme clearly had been in Grimsby during the first stage of the rising and when some of the more aggressive and impatient leaders met him and heard him suggest that they might delay proceedings until they were better organised, he was told he would be killed if he carried on in that tone.

Grimsby's final part in this dramatic tale of insurrection concerns the interception of a ship that sailed from the port towards Scarborough to help the King's men there. As the centre of gravity of the rebellion shifted to Yorkshire, where Richard Constable then moved to support Aske, the Crown's forces moved into Grimsby. Led by Charles Brandon, the King's men took Grimsby and when a ship was needed to help in Yorkshire, a man called Edward Waters set sail from Grimsby in a small craft called a crayer to help on the east coast. He and his men were boarded and taken by John Hallam and some Beverley men. They robbed Waters and did very well, even taking some guns.

In the end, the Pilgrimage of Grace failed and many men were tried and executed, including over sixty at Louth. But the beginning, in that same Wolds town and in Lincoln, was dramatic in the extreme. When the King's Messenger read out the King's truculent and harsh response to their petition against the impositions, as one man wrote at the time, he feared for his life as he wrote: 'I read the King's letter openly and because there was a little clause therein that would stir the Commons, I did leave that clause unread . . . because I was like to be slain.'

# CHAPTER 5

# Crime in the Countryside during the 1830s

## Sheep-stealing was an offence that had sent hundreds to the gallows

I n 1831, a judge in Salisbury sent twenty-five men to be hanged. One prisoner had assaulted an officer of the parish and the others were involved in a riot. One newspaper report said: 'On the men leaving the court a most distressing scene occurred. Their wives, their mothers, their sisters, and their children clung around them and the prisoners wept like infants.' This account was typical of a decade in which fear and criminality raged across the land like a forest fire, and Lincolnshire shuddered like every other county.

In Lincoln, in the same year, rioting broke out near Sawtry and spread across into Northamptonshire. What was happening became a terror across the Eastern counties, known as the 'Captain Swing' crime wave. These events took their name from riots that began in Eastkentans and spread widely, spurred by low wages and desperately poor conditions for all farm workers. Threatening letters that were sent to farmers were signed 'Captain Swing' (a reference to swinging on the gallows). Obviously, the nickname created a certain shiver of apprehension in the wealthier people and that fear extended as far as Grimsby and in particular to the areas around Waltham and Laceby where large and open villages were susceptible to such attacks and crime. The main offences were rick-burning, animal-maiming and sheep-stealing.

The men who committed the offences were running a high risk. Sheep-stealing was an offence that had sent hundreds to the gallows. But in most cases in these villages, the land was marsh-land pasture settled by small landholders, and of course they would be vulnerable and would look to the magistrates' courts to protect them. In one village, Bradley Haverstoe, court records

# *Ten*
# GUINEAS
# REWARD.

**WHEREAS** some evil disposed person or persons have lately

# *Disfigured*

### SEVERAL VALUABLE

# HORSES,

The Property of **RICHARD NAINBY, ESQ.**, on his Farm and Premises at **BARNOLDBY-LE-BECK**, by pulling large quantities of Hair from their Manes and Tails.

## *Notice is hereby given,*

That whoever will give such Information as will lead to the Discovery of the Offender or Offenders, shall, on Conviction, receive a Reward of **TEN GUINEAS** from the said **RICHARD NAINBY**.

BARNOLDBY-LE-BECK, 30th April, 1832

SKELTON, PRINTER, GRIMSBY.

Poster on the crime of
disfiguring horses.
Skelton Collection

have given us a detailed picture of what measures were taken to try to stop the terrifying attacks and burnings that were creating a profoundly difficult situation. Fortunately, a collection of hand-bills and posters issued by Skeltons, the printers, has also helped us to understand the measures taken, the rewards and indeed the nature of the fears among the landed classes.

Records from the Petty Sessions survive. These were meetings at which magistrates would gather with solicitors in Grimsby and decide on punishments. William Marshall was the Grimsby man in this group, along with the solicitor, Joseph Daubney, who kept the records. More serious offences would be dealt with at Quarter Sessions in larger towns, but the records of the Petty Sessions give us a valuable insight into how efforts were made to repress the villains and their activities. These records cover the years 1831 to 1840, so they give a good idea of the local echoes of the major national troubles going on as the agitation for the reform of the suffrage was developing, the Captain Swing problems and indeed the long-standing criminal issues linked with the repressive Game Acts.

There was clearly deep-seated hatred and resentment from the workers, as one offence shows. A labourer called Edward Borrell wrote a threatening letter to William Keyworth who was a local constable as well as a businessman in Laceby. Borrell was traced after sending a note in which he said: 'Firing is no warning to you at Laceby; you must not try the poor so any longer . . . if you do not raise their wages you must suffer by the consequence.' As a measure of just how tough the law was at that time, we have to note that Borrell was sentenced to transportation for life after his appearance at the Assizes. But other offences were regular occurrences, such as horses being maimed and corn-stacks set on fire. In an effort to let solidarity do its part as well as the usual legal measures, Bradley Haverstoe created a self-help group called an Association for the Prosecution of Felons. This meant that villains would be aware that there was a sense of unity on their

# FIVE
# *Sovereigns*
# REWARD.

**WHEREAS the WALL IN FRONT OF THE HALL, in WALTHAM, belonging to BUSHELL ANNINGSON, Esq., has of late been wantonly and maliciously THROWN DOWN and DESTROYED.**

# Notice is hereby given,

**That any Person who will give such Information to me, as that the Offender or Offenders may be proceeded against according to Law, shall receive the above Reward.**

## JOSEPH DAUBNEY.

Great Grimsby, 24th Feb., 1834.

SKELTON, PRINTER, GRIMSBY.

Reward poster. Skelton Collection

# FULL AND CORRECT

# SENTENCES

## OF THE PRISONERS
### For the Lincolnshire Summer Assizes,

Holden at the Castle of Lincoln, in and for the County of Lincoln, on Saturday the Sixteenth day of July, 1831, before the Right Honorable SIR NICHOLAS CONYNGHAM TINDAL, Chief Justice of our Lord the King, of his Court of Common Pleas; and the Honorable Sir JOSEPH LITTLEDALE, Knight, one of the Justices of our said Lord the King, assigned to hold pleas before the King himself.

## *Henry Bacon Hickman, Esq. Sheriff.*

1.  *William Wells*, aged 31, committed March 14, 1831, charged on the oath of John Parish Campbell, of Hackthorn, farmer, and others, with having on the 23rd of Nov. last, together with another person unknown, violently assaulted the said J. P. Campbell, and robbing him of 3½d on the king's highway. in the parish of Louth. *Not Guilty.*
2.  *William Barber*, aged 23, late of Ropsley. laborer, com. March 14th, 1831, charged with having wilfully, maliciously, and feloniously set fire to and burnt part of a Bean Stack, and a Clover Seed Stack, the property of W. Guylee, of Ropsley aforesaid.  *No Bill.*
3.  *James Chambers*, aged 51, laborer. com. March 1831, charged on the oath of Robert Wrout, of Sutton St. Mary's, with having on the night of the 12th March, feloniously killed and slaughtered one sheep, his property. *Death recorded.*
4.  *Richard Cooling*, the younger aged 26, and ⎫ com. March 29, 1831, charged on the oath of John Cherry, of
5.  *Thomas Motley*, aged 20,                 ⎬ Stickney, and others, with having wilfully and maliciously set fire to a beast shed, containing a quantity of implements of husbandry, a cart, also a quantity of oat straw, the property of the said John Cherry, situate in the parish of Lushby. *Guilty, Death ——Ordered for Execution.*
6.  *William Blakey*, aged 26, com. April 2, 1831, charged on the oath of Thomas Walkden, of Barton, with feloniously stealing from the Steam Packet called the Waterloo, a parcel containing among other things a bill of Exchange for 100l.  *Not Guilty.*
7.  *George Denman*, aged 35, com. April 26, charged with feloniously and sacrilegiously breaking open and entering the Church at Market Deeping, during the night of the 22nd of April last, and stealing thereout one brass chandelier, one velvet cushion, one yard of crimson twilled stuff one clergyman's surplice and one window blind, the property of William Goodall, Churchwarden.  *Guilty—Death recorded.*
8.  *Thomas Wells*, aged 28, late of Spittlegate, com May 12, charged with feloniously assaulting William Wing, of Denton, and stealing from his person a watch. *Guilty—Death recorded.*
9.  *Thomas Codd*, aged 58. com. May 20, charged with having maliciously and feloniously stabbed Jacob Richardson, of Mumby cum Chapel, with intent to kill him or to do him some grievous bodily harm. *Guilty,—Death recorded,*
10. *George Farrow*, aged 22, late of Melton Ross, near Barton, com. June 4th, charged upon the oath of Elizabeth Roberts, with feloniously administering poison to Fanny Roberts, her infant daughter. *Guilty of the attempt, Death reco.*
11. *John Edwards*, aged 25, com. June 23, charged on the oath of the said John Dewey, of Bourn, with having feloniously slaughtered and stole one lamb, the property of the said John Dewey.  *Guilty –Death recorded.*
12. *James Hargrave*, aged 28, late of Sutton St. Mary's com. July 4th, charged on the oath of ——— Lovitt, a Shepherd, with stealing a two-shear-wether sheep, on the 10th June, the property of W. Thompson.  *Death recorded.*
13. *William Hall*, aged 22, late of Grimsby, com. July 4th, charged with the wilful murder of Edward Button, on the night of the 2nd instant, by stabbing him with a knife at Grimsby aforesaid. *Guilty—Death, to be executed on Friday*
14. *Christopher Maxey*, aged 20, convicted last assizes with setting fire to a stack of mustard seed straw, at Lutton, to be brought up this assizes to receive sentence. *Discharged.*
15. *William Harness*, com. after the commencement of the Assizes, charged with stabbing a pig, at Horncastle on Saturday night last, July 16th, the property of Mr. Brunney.  *Acquitted.*

## PRISONERS IN THE CITY GOAL.

1.  *Thomas Wood*, aged 22, ⎫ late of the parish of St. Martin, charged upon the oath of Henry Stanley,  Boot and
2.  *John Wood*, aged 31, and ⎬ Shoe dealer, with having in the night of the 19th June last, burglariously broken into
3.  *John Robinson*, aged 23, ⎭ his dwelling house, and feloniously stealing therefrom 156 pairs of Shoes, and 27 pairs of Boots, the property of the said Henry Stanley.     *Robinson not guilty.    Other two, Guilty, Death recorded.*

KEYWORTH PRINTER. LINCOLN,

Sentence Lists from 1831. Author's collection

intended victims. So active and determined were the local traders and farmers in their efforts to protect themselves that they were alarmed by a tramp who was taken in for merely saying that 'it was a pity that more stacks were not burned'.

The really interesting clues to the fears inspired by Captain Swing and other popular revolts are in the bills printed by Skelton and, of course, in the rewards offered. For instance, £100 was the reward offered for the capture of people who had been involved in incendiarism. The bill says: 'The Committee of the Grimsby Association for the Prevention and Detection of Incendiarism offer the reward of one hundred pounds for the discovery of the person or persons who maliciously set fire to the corn-stacks of Mr Richard Faulding of Waltham . . .'

# ONE HUNDRED POUNDS REWARD.

The Committee of the GRIMSBY ASSOCIATION for the Prevention and Detection of Incendiarism, offer a Reward of ONE HUNDRED POUNDS for the Discovery of the Person or Persons who maliciously set on fire the CORN-STACKS, &c., of MR. RICHARD FAULDING, of Waltham, on Wednesday Evening the 26th of November last, to be paid on conviction of the Offender or Offenders.

BY ORDER OF THE COMMITTEE.

*Great Grimsby, Dec.* 9, 1834.

SKELTON, PRINTER, GRIMSBY.

Reward poster. Skelton Collection

# Sheep Slaughtered.

## Bradley Haverstoc, &c.

# ASSOCIATION

### FOR THE PROSECUTION OF FELONS.

## 15 GUINEAS

# REWARD

**WHEREAS** some evil disposed Person or Persons, on Saturday Night the 14th, or early on Sunday Morning the 15th of January instant, **SLAUGHTERED** a **SHEARLING WETHER SHEEP**, the Property of Mr. **WILLIAM MARSHALL**, of Humberstone, on Land in his occupation, situate at Weelsby, called BALL's LAND, and did feloniously steal, take, and carry away the Carcass, leaving the Skin, Head, and Entrails on the Land.

# NOTICE

## IS HEREBY GIVEN,

That whoever will give such Information as will lead to the Discovery of the Offender or Offenders, shall, on Conviction, receive a Reward of **TEN GUINEAS** from the said Association, and a further Reward of **FIVE GUINEAS** from the said William Marshall.

BY ORDER,

# Joseph Daubney,

*Secretary and Treasurer to the said Association.*

Great Grimsby, 18th January, 1832.

SKELTON, PRINTER, GRIMSBY.

Reward poster on sheep slaughtering. Skelton Collection

In 1830, a man had been executed in Lincoln for sheep-stealing and that was a common fear among the farmers, of course. Their only defence was to instil fear. Poor men would naturally risk their lives when it was a question of staving off the horrors of starvation in their families. But sheep were not only stolen – they were also slaughtered in acts of sheer malevolence, such was the deep hatred of the landholders. Joseph Daubney, in his capacity of secretary to the Bradley Haverstoe group, stated on one of his notices that such a horrible crime had taken place in January 1832, saying: '. . . some evil disposed person or persons on Saturday night the 14th or early on Sunday morning . . . slaughtered a shearling wether sheep, the property of Mr William Marshall of Humberstone.'

Overall, the decade was a time of terror in the rural areas and the crimes were diverse and numerous. During the decade 1830–40, there were ninety-nine cases of assault and twenty-three cases of sheep-stealing before the Bradley Haverstoe Petty Sessions. The Grimsby area was not untouched by the general fears across the country and these nasty offences show us today that it was not only the new industrial towns that felt the effects of the economic privations of the new industrialism and land enclosure. So determined were the Grimsby men to suppress these riots and attacks that there is a suggestion that they even employed a London policeman to help them – and this was only four years after the formation of the Metropolitan Police Act of Sir Robert Peel. If that is true, it is a measure of their desperation against these determined criminals of the fields and villages.

# CHAPTER 6

# Fatal Stabbing at the *Duke of York* 1831

## I'll kill Kempsley and somebody else

dward Hall liked a drink. In fact he liked to have an enormous quantity of drink, and that always led him into trouble. In July 1831, it led him to the gallows in Lincoln.

Hall, just twenty-two, was out filling himself with beer one June evening in Grimsby when he made too much noise for Edward Button, living near the alehouses where Hall had a good time. Hall was making a nuisance of himself in a pub run by a Mr Kempsley and Button came to help the landlord throw the drunkard out into the street. After Hall was turfed out, Button still kept on his case, shouting through a window: 'Take him to the gaol, the rascal deserves to go for making such a row on a Sunday night.' Button was being a good citizen, expressing his moral views openly. The problem was that Hall felt that deeply and he vowed revenge.

'I'll kill Kempsley and somebody else!' he roared as he sharpened a knife on a stone a few days later. A witness heard him make that awful oath. Milner, who spent time with Hall, monitored the progress of the man's rankling hatred of the landlord and of Button.

Nothing much happened for a few days but on 2 July, Milner went out drinking with a man called Joseph Nash and also with Edward Button. They went along to the *Duke of York*, run by a Mrs Dines, and much later on, near midnight, Hall and his friend Ratton came in. Hall was in a raucous mood, out to provoke Button and he succeeded. According to a witness, Button said: 'Hello! What do you want?'

'One bully has as much right here as another,' Hall answered, and Button followed that with a blow to Hall's face. Milner said that, at first, Button never even moved from his chair, but soon after there was a direct confrontation. Hall strode across to the far

## Trial and Execution of William Hall, for the
# MURDER OF EDWARD BUTTON,
### AT GRIMSBY. Executed at Lincoln, July 22, 1831.

WILLIAM HALL, a young man, scarcely attained the age 22 years, when he was convicted for the wilful murder of Edward Button, under the following circumstances: it was clearly proved on the trial that Hall was intoxicated on the Sunday, (a week previous to the murder being committed) and that Button had assisted in putting him out of a public house kept by Mr. Kempsley, where he was making a disturbance, after he was turned out Button said through the window, "take him to the goal, the rascal deserves to go for making such a row on a Sunday night," from this it appears that Hall took offence, and vowed he would have revenge if it was seven years first; one witness swore to having seen him on the Wednesday sharpening a knife on a stone, and again on Thursday he see him sharpening the same knife on a stone trough in Mrs. Dines' yard, it was a small pointed shut knife, with a bone haft, he sharpened the point of it. When he had done his knife he swore he would kill Kempsley and somebody else, but he did not say who: he said "I'll kill Kempsley and somebody else," it was about dusk, the knife might be four inches altogether; from this time to the night of the murder nothing particular appears to have occurred. The awful murder took place at the Duke of York public house, in Grimsby, on Saturday night, July 2nd, 1831 Wm. Milner, one of the principal witnesses gave evidence to the following effect; he stated that himself, Edward Button, & Joseph Nash, went to Mrs. Dines', the Duke of York Inn, between 11 and 12 o'clock at night; William Hall came in about half an hour afterwards with Josh. Ratton; Hall was in liquor; Button said, "Hollo! what do you want," Hall replied, "One bully has as much right here as another;" Button then struck Hall, but never got from his chair; Hall walked to the far corner of the room and told him he might come on, he was ready for him; Button got up and pulled off his jacket, and they commenced fighting directly. In a short time both parties fell to the floor; they fell in the doorway leading from one room into another, there was no light in the other room, but it was not very dark where they fell. In a short time Button rose up and walked part way across the kitchen floor, and fell backwards; witness lifted him up and put him in a chair, he never spoke, gave one gasp, ground his teeth together, and died in a moment. witness thought he was in a fit. till the blood fell from his side; opened his waistcoat and saw a wound in his breast, Mrs. Dines said the man is stabbed; Hall had left the room, when he returned, witness said, "Hall you have stabbed this man with a knife," he said, "I have not; I have no knife about me," witness said, "I don't suppose you have now, you have been out of doors and thrown the knife away." In addition to the above, Mary Ann Dines, daughter of the landlady, gave the following additional evidence. Heard Hall say "come on," he had one arm behind him and the other before him, they fell partly in the other room. Witness took up a candle, they were both then on the ground, Hall had one knee on Button and the other on the floor, Hall knocked the light out of her hand, and the candle went out, but before the light was out she saw a knife in Hall's hand. The above evidence was corroborated by other witnesses.

The Surgeon who examined the body, said there was a wound on the left side of the chest, he afterwards opened the body; the wound was about two inches from the point of the sternum, it had passed through the integuments in an oblique direction, upwards and inwards, entering between the fifth and sixth ribs, perforated the peri cerdium, and entered the left verticle of the heart; the instrument must have been 3½ or 4 inches long, it was about half an inch wide: the wound must have been made by a sharp pointed instrument: there is no doubt but that the wound caused the death of the deceased: After such a wound, a man would die immediately. This being the case for the prosecution & the prisoner said he had nothing to say in his defence, the Judge summed up the evidence, & the Jury returned a verdict of *Guilty*.

His Lordship placed the black cap on his head, and in the most solemn manner remarked strongly on the premeditated malice of the prisoner's mind, in having on two separate occasions sharpened a knife with a cool & deliberate intent to use such weapon against one if not two persons; that the evidence was clear & consistent throughout; and that no other verdict could be arrived at under the circumstances. The sentence of the law is, that you be taken hence to the place from whence you came; and from thence to the place of execution, and there to be hung by the neck until you are dead, and that your body be afterwards given to the surgeons for dissection, and the Lord have mercy on your soul.

The prisoner during the whole of the trial preserved a remarkable indifference to his fate; but afterwards he manifested a very different spirit, and his demeanor after condemnation was truly becoming, neither displaying excess of timidity, nor unbecoming confidence, but looked forward to his approaching fate with calmness and resignation. On ascending the fatal tower his faith forsook him, and his cries and groans was truly heart rending. The condemned Sermon was preached on Thursday Afternoon, from GENESIS Ch. IV, v. 10. "And he said, What hast thou done? the voice of thy brother's blood crieth unto me from the ground."

On Friday, this unfortunate young man paid the forfeiture of his life on the New Drop, at the top of the Castle Walls, and being market day, a great many people assembled to witness the awful scene.

(*Keyworth, Printer, Lincoln.*)

Handbill on Hall's execution. Author's collection

corner of the inn and challenged his enemy, saying: 'I'm ready for you any time!'

A Lincoln pamphlet on the event reports the fight as being a desperate affair: 'In a short time both parties fell to the floor; they fell in the doorway leading from one room into another, there was no light in the other room, but it was not very dark where they fell . . .' What happened next must be a familiar tale from many a drunken brawl. One of the men had a knife and, of course, it was Hall. From the struggle on the floor, Button emerged, staggering into the light for all to see; then he managed to walk to a chair and sat down, clearly in great pain and bleeding. Someone

The tower at Cobb Hall, Lincoln Castle: hanging place. The author

*Strugglers Inn*, Lincoln, where Button and others would have had their last drink. The author

at the scene said that he ground his teeth together and then died instantly.

A man opened Button's waistcoat because the crowd thought he was having a fit, but then the blood was evident and the man 'saw a wound on the fellow's breast'. The landlady screamed out loud that a man had been stabbed. As for Hall, in his drink he still had the wit to try to throw away the weapon. He appears to have gone outside to do that and then go back inside the inn where someone accused him, saying: 'Hall, you have stabbed this man with a knife.' Hall said that he had no knife on him.

Naturally, everyone there knew that he had been outside to throw away the murder weapon. Later in court, the daughter of the landlady said that she heard Hall provoke Button, saying: 'Come on!' She said he had one arm behind him – that was where he held the knife. She said that she followed the fight, holding a candle, and she said that she saw Hall holding Button fast to the ground, with a knee on him, and then the killer knocked away her candle. Before the light was out, though, she said: 'I saw a knife in Hall's hand.' She was not the only one there who saw that.

Evidence from the local surgeon confirmed that Button had suffered a deep two-inch long wound by his sternum and the knife 'had passed through the integuments in an oblique direction, upwards and inwards, entering between the fifth and sixth ribs'. The doctor stated that there was no doubt that the knife-wound had caused the death of the deceased. In court, all this was heard in silence by the man in the dock, and he had nothing to say before a guilty verdict was passed on him.

The reporter in court noted that: 'The prisoner, during the whole of the trial, preserved a remarkable indifference to his fate, but afterwards he manifested a very different spirit.' That was after the judge donned the black cap and sentenced Hall to hang. The judge commented on 'the premeditated malice in the prisoner's mind, in having, on two separate occasions, sharpened a knife with a cool and deliberate intent to use such a weapon against one, if not two persons . . .'

The reporter went on, saying that Hall's behaviour was then 'truly becoming, neither displaying excess of timidity nor unbecoming confidence, but looked forward to his approaching fate with calmness and resignation'. The assembled crowd by the tower at Cobb Hall, Lincoln Castle, had what they thought was good entertainment, many paying for the best views of the hanging from the inns across the road. They even enjoyed a long sermon on the sins of the condemned man. This was on 22 July 1831, and Hall must have wished he could have had more than the traditional final drink of ale at *The Strugglers Inn* public house by the castle walls.

# CHAPTER 7

# Violence at the Elections 1862 and 1877

## The *Yarborough Hotel* was the focus for a hellish brawl . . .

Elections in the nineteenth century were invariably the scenes of riots and fights. After all, local passions ran high when strangers came in to stand for their seat and take on the local man. The local man might also be a hard landowner with entrenched conservative views who might also have been a magistrate and so would be hated by many. Allegiances were strong and found aggressive outlets whenever there was a sniff of something dramatic and sensational on the wind. In Lincoln in the 1820s there had even been a murder associated with a candidate. Then, Grimsby had several riotous elections, the worst coming in 1862 and again fifteen years later.

In 1862, just eleven years after the *Yarborough Hotel* had been built, things were improving for the town. A new railway had been constructed and the hotel had been built by the great Lord Yarborough, who was chairman of the Manchester, Sheffield and Lincolnshire Railway Company. Then, in that fateful year for local politics, a riot started there, resulting in much of the interior being wrecked; the hotel had always been a favourite spot for local businessmen to meet – in the smoke room, usually.

Trouble had been expected and police had been standing by earlier in the day, brought in from Hull. But what caused the trouble was something familiar in local elections at the time – outsiders brought in to help organise a campaign, in this case towards the Liberal candidate, Heneage. Two men from Liverpool were brought in to do this and, as they were being given a grand meal, the enemy arrived. The entire hatred seems to have been directed towards the two voters inside. Even their own sisters were in the crowd, shouting that they would 'tear their eyes out' if anyone supported Heneage. According to a contemporary account, the women were 'violent blackguards' and they were certainly talented at causing a fight. Thanks to their provocations, matters escalated and the mob attacked and the *Yarborough Hotel* was the focus for a hellish brawl. Many thought that fifty Hull policemen acted so extremely that they aggravated the situation, but whatever the cause, the result was chaos and destruction. Sixteen police officers had been inside the building, but they thought that discretion was the better part of valour and they beat a retreat. That supports the view that it was left to the Hull men to sort things out and they did so with too much vigour.

When normality was more or less restored, arrests were made and four men were given prison sentences. Naturally, after the storm and the election itself (at which Heneage lost) the loser was certain that his enemies had planned everything; a stool-pigeon called Hopkin was located and found to have voted against his employer. In the days well before the Secret Ballot Act of 1872,

The *Yarborough Hotel*, where the brawl took place. The author

# GENTLEMEN
# *Freeholders*
OF
# THE COUNTY
OF
# Lincoln!

I regret much that any advertisements should be issued to find a head for that vain silly body, which, to our own knowledge, has long been contemptible to us, and most mischievous to himself. *No head* can ever supply his body with wholesome food; *no brains* will ever be useful to him. He is a Busy Body—a perfect Marplot. He has long enjoyed the friendship of certain Lords in Yorkshire, Northamptonshire, and Lincolnshire; and never before complained of their unconstitutional kindness to him. They little knew his origin, or would not have confided in him: he was the spoilt and only son of a Quill-driver at Newark. This *body of a Heron*, without any plumage on his back, but with white feathers in his tail, and *the Witham Goose*, his *comrade*, have in a few days hatched a Syston Egg, and from it has burst, in a marvellous manner, a perfect Zany, without any feathers on his back, but a most perfect cap on his head, ornamented with musical Bells. I lament to see this woeful change arise in old Syston Park, where, fifty years ago, no mule bird was to be seen. What will become of this curiosity, time will prove—no honest Freeholder will care; most probably he will be exhibited for a season at Exeter 'Change with Witham Goose and Stubton Heron, and afterwards will be sent to the archives in Coventry, and deposited with Lady Godiva and Peeping Tom.

*AN OLD FREEHOLDER.*

*December 3rd,* 1823.

[JACKSONS, PRINTERS, LOUTH.]

Typical election poster of the time. Author's collection

this could happen. The tale was that the poor man had been plied with drink and put onto a London train.

In May 1877, another election riot damaged the *Royal Hotel*. After walking out of the House of Commons, the MP John Chapman died. He had been ill since the 1874 election and now his demise opened up new campaigns. Heneage, who was to become member for Grimsby later, declined the offer of a place on the railway board – always the marker for the 'railway seat' as it was often called. It was to create something of a mess and so the trouble followed. The 'railway candidate' became Watkin, after his approaches to Heneage and to George Morland Hutton had failed. But Watkin had made moves. When two railway secretaries arrived in Grimsby with Heneage, they saw people on the platform with banners proclaiming: 'Vote for Watkin'. The trouble this time was not as severe as in 1862 but there was certainly a fight that did some damage at the *Royal*. The police, though, now more informed and organised after learning from experience, kept trouble to a minimum. Alfred Watkin won, and Edward Heneage's turn was to come in 1880. In the meantime he had other duties, such as being appointed one of the sheriffs for Lincolnshire, in 1877. He was MP for Grimsby from 1880 to 1886, as a Liberal, and again in the years 1886–92 and 1893–98.

# CHAPTER 8

# Problems for the New Police 1850–1900

## The fishermen were generally accounted to be the worse for violence

Grimsby had its first professional police force in 1846, starting with an initial strength of four men, with Isaac Anson as the Chief. Since Peel's Police Act of 1829 and the Municipal Corporations Act of 1835, moves had been made to create a national network of police forces and Grimsby was soon well-organised in that respect. But we have to wonder at the first few years, with only a very small number of officers: they must have had a hard time.

As the century went on, though, the police reports were frequently done and they give us an insight into some of the work involved: lists of summary offences include dozens of crimes, but the most frequent and persistent were obstructions and nuisances, common assaults, drunkenness with aggravation and Sunday trading. Indictable offences had their own league table and the highest on that list was usually simple larceny.

The major influences on the police work obviously reflect social history in broader terms. By 1848, the town had a rail link with London and the overall population boomed in the mid and later Victorian years, rising to over 43,000 by 1880. The policeman's lot was certainly 'not a happy one' as Gilbert and Sullivan wrote. They were often attacked and subject to discipline. Many officers were sacked for drunkenness and taking bribes. They also had to learn to use discretion and common sense in terms of the workings of brothels and such people as vagrants and 'town characters'. Even as late as 1918, in a police handbook written by the Chief Constable of Lincolnshire, it is noticeable that there was a great deal of guidance on professional behaviour. Examples included: 'All constables are expected to take the greatest care of the uniform issued to them, it being public property', and: 'No constable is allowed to lend money to any other member of the Force. Dismissal of both borrower and lender will be the penalty for breaking this rule.'

Later in the century, policing Cleethorpes presented particular problems and duties, mainly relating to following the by-laws such as 'No person shall throw, place or leave any orange peel, banana skin or other dangerous substance on any footway'.

Satire on the new Police Act of 1829. Clifford Elmer

George Stennett, Assistant
Chief Constable of
Lincolnshire, 1901-1908.
Lincolnshire Archives

Far more important was the subject of the officers' vulnerability. They were often attacked, as in 1858 when a gang of fishermen set about a constable on his beat. In terms of serious crime, in the period 1880–81, 1,672 people were subject to criminal proceedings. The fishermen were generally accounted to be the worst for violence. The author of the standard history of the town notes that they were, 'violent, immoral and in some cases well able to tempt the police with bribes'. Yet the public still complained, as one letter-writer cavilled in 1850 who wrote that in a walk at night he saw 'six policemen in want of a job'.

As in the case of the *Yarborough Hotel* in the 1862 election, police from further afield were drafted in when needed. It took decades for a fully professional force to be regulated and supervised. On the way to that achievement were such events as the career of Sergeant Hardcastle, who was told he could be dispensed with just nine months after being appointed, but (as there was a shortage of suitable men) stayed on and was sacked for insubordination in 1860. By 1878, the force was experimenting with plain clothes men (there had been a central detective force in London since 1842). But as is often the case, criminals changed and removed themselves to counteract such moves. Citizens had to learn to use the police expertise as well, as in the case of one of hundreds of crimes committed at the Grimsby market, when a pickpocket was arrested in 1868. A woman told Sergeant Allbones that a pickpocket was at work and he watched and arrested two men, Fielding and Watson. Clearly, the profession was becoming a real presence by that date.

Five Chief Constables, after Anson, were in for a tough time.

# CHAPTER 9

# Neglect on a Train
# 1860

## The idea of negligence seemed to be a new concept

There is no doubt that some foul deeds are not done with a purposeful desire to do someone or something harm. But, nevertheless, painful and often tragic consequences can follow a piece of bungling in public service or even in relationships in a neighbourhood. This applies to a case against the Manchester, Sheffield and Lincolnshire Railway in which a passenger had a very hard time. The problem was that at the time the idea of negligence was a new concept.

There was a rich assembly of barristers on the Midland Circuit on 19 March 1862, to hear what had happened to Mr Burgess, a butcher and cattle dealer, as he boarded a train for Grimsby after attending the Wakefield cattle market on Boxing Day 1860. He was roughing it, travelling third class, and at that time trains were still something fairly new, so the notion of comfort was still in progress as well. Burgess had to change trains at East Retford and he went into a carriage next to the break-van, as was the normal way. He went into the middle compartment of three, together with six other passengers. That was just the beginning of his adventure.

An important detail here was that the communication cord, leading from Burgess's carriage to the break-van, had been taken out for some reason. The first stage of the journey was fine, stopping at Gainsborough and then on to Blyton. But there was snow on the line and the train was losing time; it was also snowing intensely. That snow was gathering deeply on the railway line.

Then the problems began. *The Times* reported the beginnings of the awful events of that night: 'Soon after the train started the passengers in the last carriage perceived that it swayed with a very irregular motion, which increased as it proceeded; the doors were flung open, the lamp above them fell onto the floor, and it was soon perceived that a wheel of which the tyre was broken, had gone off the axle.' After that, the whole body of the carriage toppled and it trailed along the ground. The unfortunate passengers had to cling on for dear life, grasping anything they could to hold on to.

The door of the carriage and some of the sides, were then broken and flapping; there was debris falling on the people. Everyone else had fallen off before Burgess: he fell heavily and his head was wounded. Somehow, he and the others managed to get to their feet and walked back to Gainsborough from Blyton. A doctor was fetched for him as he arrived in a pitiable condition at the *White Hart* inn. It was two days before he could get back home to Grimsby. Burgess was very ill for a month, confined to bed by his doctor.

He prosecuted the firm for negligence, the cause being that the break-van was at the engine side of the carriage, so the end-carriage was most vulnerable in the event of an accident. It was Boxing Day, so staff may have been enjoying their beers too freely. But the Company argued in court that there was simply a problem with one wheel. They said that the frost caused the tyre to burst, and argued that they could not have kept a watchful eye on the passengers had they been placed in any carriage – unless guards had kept their bodies outstretched from the windows on the entire journey north.

The barrister defending the Company reasoned that there should be a considerable reduction in the amount of the damages claimed. What at first appeared to be on the side of the Company (after their lawyer had done his homework well) was that Burgess had suffered a stroke in 1857. This gave them leeway to claim that the man had a weak constitution regardless of what had happened that night. For Burgess, his lawyer, Sergeant Hayes, gave a logical and very emotional response but it was left to the judge, the Lord Chief Justice, Mr Williams, to advise the jury. He made it clear that there were weaknesses in the defences put forward by the Company. Burgess was awarded £100 damages, which was a large sum in those days.

The Company were always having such problems with passengers in that decade. In the same year, a young woman was travelling from Hull to Grimsby to see her uncle when, between Haborough and Stallingborough, the carriage she was in 'oscillated very much'. The woman was taken off the train after her legs went completely numb and taken to Grimsby on a special train. She appears to have made a claim for damages after the contraction of bronchitis, but the harm done to one of her knees by the action of the engine was the main concern. The defence was that a spring had broken in the engine – and that there was no material defect in its construction.

It must have seemed as though the Company would win that case, as it was not difficult to show that the plaintiff had a 'weak constitution' but what happened was that the defence demonstrated rather too aggressively that her injury was really severe because she delayed taking medical advice. With a young woman apparently crippled in front of them looking pathetically weak alongside the wealthy and well-fed representatives of a major transport company, the jury found for the plaintiff. In other words, the young woman was awarded the huge sum of £400 damages. What turned events in the courtroom into her favour was the discovery that the inspector, the man who should have examined the keys in the chairs before departure, had not done so. The reporter told his public at the time that 'Many of the keys supposed to have been displaced were not really so, but were new keys, purposely not driven home into the chairs.'

The heart of the problem was not the engine, but the very chairs that the passengers had sat on. Naturally, a frail woman at the mercy of such vibrations would suffer great pain. It all makes sense today, in our world of hyper-sensitive customer care and rigid Health and Safety legislation but, in 1862, they were just beginning to learn the folly of neglecting such things. The Manchester, Sheffield and Lincolnshire Railway Company had a lot to learn. Running a railway, they were discovering, meant much more than attaching carriages to a locomotive and heading in the right direction.

# CHAPTER 10

# Rape on the Dock
# 1866

## A police officer saw the attack and walked away . . .

Sexual assault and rape in the nineteenth century presented particular difficulties for the law machine. When a case did actually reach a courtroom the result was often severe. Between 1814 and 1834, 166 men were convicted of rape or extreme sexual assault and seventy-nine of these were executed. Prostitution was so common that often people were desensitised to the notion of a couple having sex in some dark corner. In Grimsby, brothels ran a very successful trade in the Victorian period and police officers were often in the unenviable position of not being sure whether an action was a sexual assault or a 'lady of the night' with a client. But all this is no excuse for what happened on 13 May 1866, near the dock offices.

Lucy Sizer was only sixteen when she walked to the chapel service on that date, her little sister with her. They went to the evening service, but it was still light when they walked home, and they were accosted by the offices at the dock by a man called Crawford. The younger sister was a problem and the ruffian did his best to instil fear into the little girl by pushing her way. She would not budge, though, and he had to give her money before he could get hold of Lucy and have his wicked way with her. With the youngster out of the way, the man hauled his victim off to a shed in the railway yards where his accomplices were waiting. With his hand over her mouth, he roughly forced her into the place and he and four other men gang-raped the poor girl.

It is stunning to read about the other events around the attack, most notably the behaviour of a man of law who was near. It is disgusting to relate that a police officer saw the attack and walked away. Violence and gang crime was so common that the constables were sometimes frightened and at other times bored and frustrated by the regular occurrence of violence and gang fights in the area.

Lucy was helped away after the attack, as she was badly shaken and in profound mental distress. But it was not difficult to catch the perpetrators as she knew one of her attackers. He was called White and he gave the names of the other men. The five were in the dock and the usual defence was raised i.e. that Lucy Sizer was on the game, or at least indulging in part-time sexual activities to supplement her meagre income. But there was so much evidence of the harm and terror done to the young girl that convictions were severe. All five men were convicted and given custodial sentences, with the leader, Crawford, given fifteen years of penal servitude. The others were given six years. An important factor was that the girl was returning from a religious service. This clearly had an impact on the judgement as it helped the judge and jury to assess her character.

Had this crime happened a decade earlier, they would have been given a sentence of transportation for life. The 1853 and 1857 Penal Servitude Acts introduced this punishment in place of a life spent in Van Dieman's Land. The new acts could give periods of servitude ranging from three years to life. Crawford's fate was very severe when we think of the rather lax views on sexual assault at the time.

Not only had the leader succeeded in his evil designs on the teenager but he had also terrified the little sister and then acted as procurer for younger men. Every angle on which we look at this awful attack presents us with more depths of depravity and Crawford's fate seems entirely appropriate. He would have been physically wrecked by his sentence and, we hope, also mentally punished as well, suffering an ordeal that might compare with that experienced by his victim.

In Grimsby in this period, convictions were very rare in this context. During the years 1860–61 and 1880–81 there was only one conviction for rape, and even at the turn of the century in many of the police returns of statistics there are very few convictions. In 1901, under the category 'indecent assaults of females' there are only four crimes 'known to the police' and it has to be said that all four were convicted.

Through the eyes of citizens wanting to encourage the idea of the prevention rather than the punishment of crime, there was certainly a desire in the community to see the police officer punished in some way.

# CHAPTER 11

# Brutal Murder of a Wife 1887

## The Grimsby fisherman was just one more face in front of him who deserved to die . . .

Mr Justice Field, a judge very busy on the Midland Circuit, arrived in Lincoln for the Assizes in 1887 fresh from a number of murder trials on the 'road' as a busy judge. Field was well-known for his tough, no nonsense attitudes to the implementation of the worst sentences of the law, and now he was to preside over the trial of a Grimsby man. He was then seventy-four and age had certainly not softened his character. The Judge had not been called to the Bar until he was thirty-seven and it could be said that he was determined to make his mark. In his long career he was involved in several high-profile cases and the small matter of yet another working man who murdered his wife was not going to trouble him.

Mr Harris, defending the accused, Richard Insole, knew that he had a difficult task. It was an uncomplicated case. Insole, a fisherman, had been separated from his wife, Sarah, since July the previous year. Sarah had gone back to live with her parents and was earning a wage. Insole had a set intention to take her life, such was his hatred of her. He bought a revolver and cartridges on 7 January 1887 and, at around ten in the morning, he appeared at Sarah's parents' home. Insole went inside the house and started a row.

The couple had a furious interchange of anger and accusation, and eventually Insole fired a shot at his wife, but she managed to raise a hand and knock his hand so that the bullet went high and wide of her. But Insole was determined and he shot again, this time hitting Sarah in the chest and she fell back into a chair. He was still not finished, firing again, but this time into the floor instead. Insole saw in that split-second that there was no going back. Still in a rage, he was interrupted by the arrival of his wife's

Executioner Calcraft.
*Author's collection*

mother who he shoved roughly away before putting the barrel of the gun next to Sarah's heart and firing twice. She died almost instantly, and he ran off. Insole was tracked down without any difficulty and, at his own home, he was arrested and detained.

The defence lawyer argued that Insole had been desperately jealous and in that state had been totally distracted, therefore not at all his normal self. As *The Times* reported the case, Harris had admitted defeat really, as he said that: 'he could not contend that there were any circumstances which would reduce the offence to manslaughter' and that he still thought that the introduction of the notion of jealousy would help the jury see his client in 'a favourable light'. He was backing a loser. Yet it must be recorded that Harris's speech achieved one thing – it guided the jury to suggest a recommendation for mercy after a guilty verdict. They had been convinced by the account of Sarah's affair with another man.

But Mr Justice Field was ready with his black cap again. His jury had actually used the word *provocation* when they asked for mercy. In 1887, that was a word with no weight at all in a case where a killer had patently had a planned intention to take life. He bought the gun and bullets, went to Sarah's home, roughly assaulted her mother, and fired the gun with a definite intention to kill. The death sentence was passed on him and Justice Field did repeat the recommendation to mercy, but it was, as he well knew, futile.

In Grimsby, however, a sufficiently large number of people

The Lucy Tower, Lincoln - graveyard of murderers. The author

Sidney Merrill showing
Marwood's hanging
rope. Author's collection

felt that they should sign a petition to save Insole's life. On 12 February, that petition was noted in the newspapers: 'A petition is being signed that the capital sentence passed upon Richard Insole the Grimsby murderer be commuted to penal servitude for life.' It was fruitless, and on Monday 24 February, at the new prison on Greetwell Road, Lincoln, the Bradford executioner James Berry arrived to see Insole into the next world.

In Berry's memoirs, a book in which many of his victims were given a few pages of detail regarding their exits, it is noticeable that Richard Insole spoke no more than a few last words. The fact he wishes to note is that Insole fired the gun for the last time as Sarah was lying on the ground. He must have formed an opinion of the killer that was so low that he took a certain pleasure in hanging Insole that day in Lincoln.

James Berry had another appointment the next day, in Nottingham, where another young wife killer was waiting to step up the scaffold to the very professionally prepared noose. This was Benjamin Terry – a man sentenced by Mr Justice Field, who was so accustomed to putting on the black cap that one distracted Grimsby fisherman was just one more face in front of him who deserved to die.

# CHAPTER 12

# Hard Labour for Oyster Stealing 1887

## Rescue the boy from the taint of prison . . .

This is a case in which it is easy to see the magistrates as the villains. They were in a mood to set an example one summer day in August when the workers of the Victorian industrial towns came to the seaside for a rest and some fun. But for one young man and his parents their day in Cleethorpes was to be disastrous, and it stirred up the lawyers around the place.

George Butterley was a boy from a good family who enjoyed an excursion to Cleethorpes – that is until he decided to take nine oysters from a box on the beach. The consequences of that small but rash act were that first he stood in front of the bench at Grimsby Police Court and then that he was sentenced to a month's hard labour. But from that small and apparently insignificant event the story goes to the House of Commons.

There, on 17 August 1887, Mr Vincent asked the Secretary of State whether or not his Honour knew about the Butterley case. Clearly, the important man did not. Mr Vincent had to spell it out for the House. The Bench at Grimsby had acted in ignorance of a new law. Just a week before young George stood in the dock the Probation of First Offenders Act had been passed. Vincent asked the Secretary to remit the sentence immediately and his argument highlights the changes in thought that were going on at the time about juvenile crime. He said that there should be a remission 'upon such conditions as might be desirable with a view of rescuing the boy from the present and future consequences of the taint of prison'. Mr Vincent was successful in his plea.

George's story highlights the difficulties that local magistrates were having in the Victorian period coping with issues of punishment for young people. As far back as 1840 a Juvenile Offenders Bill had looked at the problem of holding petty sessions in public houses. The politician involved wanted to create 'an intermediate tribunal between the magistrates and the superior courts in order to prevent young persons of 10, 11 and 12 years of age . . . from being sent to prison for first and trivial offences'. Clearly, in Grimsby, that move, forty-seven years before George's theft, counted for nothing.

The struggle throughout the century to prevent young offenders from being tainted by having time with hardened criminals went on until the landmark act of 1887 when the notion of proper probationary measures was understood and backed. Mr and Mrs Butterley had no idea that their son had caused such a stir in Grimsby that the Bench saw that they were in the wrong. The 1887 act had introduced probation into English law for the first time. Crime rate fell by 42% between 1862 and 1900, so it may have had some kind of effect.

What explains the actions taken by the Grimsby Police Court is that regions were still embedded in old ways and, before the 1880s, only notable individuals had tried to change things. An example of this concerned Frederick Rainer who saw that a large number of drunks (many young people) were appearing in London police courts. Rainer set about forming the police court missionary, a forerunner of the probation officer.

Cleethorpes c.1920 Author's collection

The 1887 legislation brought in organised supervision for young boys like George Butterley. This was the notion of friendly supervision with regular reports by the offender. There would still be reports to the court. George, after his release, had to have an account of his future conduct reported to Grimsby, so his poor parents were still not free of the long arm of the law and of the overbearing officialdom associated with the paperwork of summary courts. Nationally, the problem of what to do with the thousands of young offenders like George was still there, as it was left to courts to follow up probationary decisions.

The story of the stolen oysters meant 'egg on the face' for the Grimsby Bench, terror for young George and a long painful confrontation with the law for the couple from Sheffield. In today's terms, what the child did was the equivalent of a young-ster stealing a bar of chocolate today. But in defence of the Grimsby magistrates, it has to be noted that 'simple and minor larcenies' were running at the rate of around 270 cases a year.

# CHAPTER 13

# Cigars in the Death Cell
# 1893

## Rumbold could face death if he could just have a smoke . . .

This is the tale of a Grimsby mariner who, while waiting for execution in Lincoln Prison, wanted to get something off his chest. It was a confession of a crime he had done that was nothing to do with the reason he was in the execution cell. This was a story of him ramming and sinking a fishing boat of a company that was in competition with another. He had never said anything about this to anyone and he had been well paid for that ruthless job.

Henry Rumbold, thirty-seven, was a captain of a fishing smack working from Grimsby. He was married but was fond of other female company, and that was not hard to find around the docks. He started spending time with a woman thirteen years younger than him, Harriet Rushby. The skipper was not simply after a rough time with a lady of the night, however. He tried to play what we might call today the role of 'sugar daddy' – but with a touch of style and dignity.

Henry thought that Harriet – if she were to be available to him when he was back from sea and he wanted some entertainment outside the marriage bed – should be well-housed and looked after. He provided her with somewhere to lodge, but it wasn't enough for her. She felt the exciting pull of the pubs and the musical entertainment too much. She also liked spending time with a variety of men. She was young and attractive and men wanted her. When Henry came home and went to visit her, Harriet was not where she was meant to be, and she never had been.

This is a tale of possession. Rumbold wanted to add her to his list of property. He thought that a man with some kind of status in the community should have a mistress, and a decent one at that. When she didn't turn out to be the woman he wanted he took it into his head to go looking for her – with a gun in his hand. Rumbold searched the streets, working his way through noisy drunks and street brawls, and eventually found her in one of the night-time crowds. He had the gun out and was in a rage. Harriet was grabbed and taken to the upstairs room of her lodging house. Rumbold yelled for the other hangers-on to keep their distance. No one felt brave enough to try to protect the girl.

The crowd outside heard the girl say: 'Don't murder me Harry, in my sins!' After that outburst, a gunshot rang out in the evening air. He had killed her and then coolly stepped outside and walked away into the night, with blood visible on his hand as he stood in the doorway, as witnesses later said. He was not concerned about there being witnesses at all. It was all a matter of a murderous passion and there was no logic in his head that night. Rumbold was a man on the edge of reason and he knew that the only thing left was to end his life but, he claimed later at the trial, his weapon had malfunctioned when he tried to shoot

Lincoln Prison (built 1872). *The author*

James Billington,
hangman. The author

himself in the head. In desperation, he walked to the nearest
police officer and confessed.

The sugar daddy in the dock at Lincoln listened while the tale
of his lavish spending on the young woman was related. He had
treated her very well and he had snapped when she turned out to
be a bitter disappointment to him. There was a feeble attempt at
claiming manslaughter (as there always was in these cases) but
on very flimsy grounds. Rumbold was charged with murder and
his response was that it was right that he should die. 'Of course I
killed her,' he said, 'and I hope when I die I shall join the girl
I shot.'

But before the black cap was on the judge's head, the prisoner
was asked if he wished to speak. Rumbold then made a strange
request: he asked for a supply of cigars enough to last him for his

last three weeks of life in Lincoln Prison. The judge indulged him and let it happen. He smoked himself into a state of agitation before he walked to the scaffold on 19 December 1893, where James Billington was waiting to stretch his neck. Perhaps Henry Rumbold was fortunate at having Billington, in that the hangman had worked on reducing the time spent pinioning his victims from minutes down to just a few seconds. The hangman with the nickname of 'Jimmy Armhole' would help Henry to leave this life speedily. Just a year before his work in Lincoln, Billington had hanged the notorious poisoner, Neil Cream.

What about Rumbold's other adventure on the wrong side of the law? Henry Rumbold (called Rumbell in the report) had been involved in a case in which a smack called the *Fortuna* belonging to an alderman of Grimsby, Henry Smethurst, had been rammed and sunk by the *Ibis* after a collision. The claim was that the collision had been caused by Henry, who was master of the *Ibis* and they also said, as *The Times* reported, that 'the plaintiff Smethurst had incited and procured Rumbell to sink the *Fortuna*'.

Whatever the truth of the matter, Henry was certainly a man not to be crossed and his temper was destined to lead him to the gallows – and that was the killer's destination after he stubbed out the last of his cigars.

# Chapter 14

# Fraud and Cruelty: Extreme Crimes at the Century's End

## Three great wounds were inflicted on the lad . . .

Looking at the Chief Constable's returns as he assessed the state of law and order in late Victorian Grimsby, we have the usual predominance of every summary offence, including drunken arguments, disturbances of the peace and petty larcenies. But the last decades of the century saw some crimes that show exactly what extremes villains would go to in order to attract the attention of the law – and to run risks.

Two stories illustrate this well. One is a terribly violent series of assaults on a youth and the other a bizarre attempt to swindle a man in power. The first crime reminds us that not every 'foul deed' involves murder or extreme violence. It is, indeed, a strange tale, beginning with the Mayor of Grimsby answering the telephone and arranging an interview with a man who called himself 'Prince Makaroo'. The voice on the phone said that he (Makaroo) was a relative of King Menelek, a Zulu tribesman. The conversation must have implied a certain plausibility on the part of the caller because the Mayor agreed to an interview.

When they met, the black person who arrived spun the story of his royalty and said that he had come from Hamburg and was on his way to London. He told the Mayor that his royal servants were waiting for him in London – along with his finances. Then came the 'sting' of the fraud: the 'prince' asked for a loan and that was going too far. The police were called. All this, almost believed, even to the point of 'Makaroo' producing a passport supposedly endorsed by Sir Frank Lascelles, a well-known politician at the time.

Detective Inspector Baglee, when he arrived, knew exactly who the inept conman was. He was a man known variously as

'Khaki Jim' and 'Khaki Brown' and who had also tried to pass himself off as an Army captain in previous exploits. Such was the boldness and ingenuity of this imposter that he had written to newspapers in London with the information that 'Prince Makaroo' would be arriving in the city. He had then taken a room at a Grimsby hotel and it was even recorded that he had rung Buckingham Palace and asked to talk to King Edward.

What emerged from all this high comedy was that 'Makaroo' had been in hospital in Berlin and, on his release, the Consul had paid for his passage to Grimsby. The outcome was that he was remanded for a week and was clearly in need of medical help.

At the other extreme, the year 1885 was also the time when one of the worst ever crimes of brutality was committed on board a ship. James Gloody was skipper of the smack, *Friend* – and never was a craft more paradoxically misnamed. At the first investigation into the death of nineteen-year-old John Smith a terrible story of merciless and inhuman cruelty unfolded.

Young Smith was described in the papers as one of a class of 'waifs, who, coming to Grimsby from all parts, linger about the

The Town Hall, Grimsby. The author

# County Borough of Great Grimsby.

# CRIMINAL STATISTICS

AND

# MISCELLANEOUS RETURNS

FOR THE

## YEAR ENDED 31ST DECEMBER, 1911.

GREAT GRIMSBY:

ROBERTS & JACKSON, PRINTERS & STATIONERS, 4 VICTORIA STREET.

1912.

Title page of Criminal Statistics from 1911. Author's collection

fish docks ready for any job that may turn up'. Smith was at the
end of his tether – apparently a deserter from the army – and he
said that he did not care what happened to him. These were
horribly fateful words, because he was about to let himself be
taken in charge by a powerful sadist.

The boy Smith was taken on as a cook. But at first it was
himself who seemed to be the problem, according to later state-
ments. Smith opened a clasp-knife and acted strangely and
aggressively, so much so that some of the crew feared for their
lives. At least, that was the tale told in court. But skipper Gloody
was not one to hold back. He tended to sort out problems with
speed and incisive finality. On this occasion he grabbed an axe,
told a mate to take a spike and attack the boy with it; when that
did not happen, Gloody hit the lad with the axe. The crew testified that the skipper completely lost his head after that and began
striking the boy (then lying on the deck) fifteen times with the
weapon. The boy had, witnesses said, put his own knife away.

It is amazing to relate that young Smith was not dead at that
point, and even more disgusting to note that his awful wounds
were merely soaked in salt water. Gloody then forced the boy to
do some work. How the lad even managed to get to his feet is
beyond comprehension.

The brutal tale ended with Smith, at half past eight at night,
throwing himself into the sea. Gloody was eventually remanded
in custody for 'causing the death' of the boy. That meant
manslaughter.

The statistics of those thirty years from around 1880 to 1910
hide stories such as those recounted above. There are many
more, but these two open up some kind of understanding of the
range of crimes the police had to cope with. They have, of
course, one thing in common: both criminals were undoubtedly
utterly insane.

# CHAPTER 15

# Apprentices, Hard Times and Lincoln Gaol 1850–1900

## Lincoln rings with indignation at the treatment these lads receive

 fishing industry needs skilled men and so it always has to have recruits. The ancient apprenticeship system, applied to most important British industries, was crucially important for Grimsby. The problem was that it was hard to get the right kinds of boys – and even harder to retain them. Throughout the nineteenth century there were recurrent difficulties with employment in the fishing industry and the law. At the heart of the malfunction of the system was the fact that the industry did not usually house apprentices with masters in lodgings when they were not at sea. Instead, the boys were subject to all the usual temptations and abuses that the seaman ashore experiences.

But there was also the cyclical process of punishing apprentices who ran away from their indentures due to the hardships involved and then imprisoning them in Lincoln until they would, in many cases, return to Grimsby. The industry was totally reliant on apprentices and on the supply of boys. The young men who did live as traditional apprentices, with parents, would earn a wage and it would be used well. Otherwise, the boys who were subject to the whims of the masters would inevitably drift into crime.

In 1877, there were 1,794 apprentices and 1,676 men. Ideally, there should have been far more of the former, as around 2,500 were needed to staff the ships to optimum strength. What was going wrong was that boys were left to themselves too often, as various inquiries discovered as the century wore on. A Board of Trade inquiry, led by Swanson and Stoneham, summed up the attitudes of the skippers: 'In too many cases he [the apprentice] would appear to be regarded as merely part of the machinery for taking fish.' What started to happen was, since guardians of the poor law were less keen to send boys to Grimsby, recruitment accelerated at reformatories. For instance, reformatories in Leicestershire took 'bad lads' from Liverpool and tried to instil a religious regime. Others were to handle 'problem children' from areas nearer home. All would be recruits, even from as far away as Essex.

In this episode of Grimsby history, we need to ask who was breaking the law. The newspapers at the time put the blame on the masters. So critical were these accounts of cruelty and neglect that, in 1876, only a tiny percentage of boys indentured came from workhouses. What happened was that reformatory boys, coming to work and having no moral guidance or any kind of supervision, crossed the line into criminality. The *Grimsby Observer* complained: 'It is useless to disguise that many mere boys are tempted away to their ruin and that night after night they are absent from their lodgings, and are kept in hiding by prostitutes until discovered by the police.'

In this unsavoury climate it is a simple matter to see what the consequences would be. Petty crime, boys on the run and then prison sentences were common. At that time, Lincoln Prison (built in 1872) was taking children as well as women, so gangs of lads would appear in Lincoln, chained together and led up the High Street to the gaol by a constable. Grimsby was creating a criminal 'chain' of cause and effect, resulting in a production line of hardened crooks who would eventually have nothing to do with the fishing industry at all. The reports made it clear that, for many boys, Lincoln Prison (informally called 'Lincoln College') was preferable to a life at sea in which they had a high risk of being beaten and drowned. The risk of dying at sea was high. In 1890, for instance, 127 people were lost, and most of these fatalities were a result of poor training. Some reports stressed the physical abuse boys received, such as a statement given by Isaac Miller at the Fisherlands Institute, that he had seen boys with swollen eyes caused by beatings; and one boy had had his face rubbed with herring-heads and whipped. Later in the century, after some attempts at reform, boys were sent to Hull Prison.

In December 1881, the case of the murder of William Papper, by Oswald Brand, in Hull, had an impact on how the world in general saw skippers and apprentices working off the Humber. As the masters and skippers relied on the criminal justice system to support them and help maintain the supply of boys, Hull and

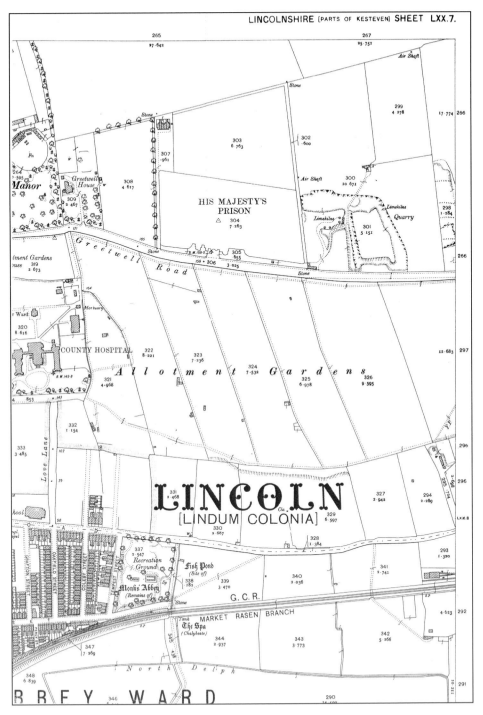

Lincoln Prison on the 1903 Ordnance Survey (note the limekilns nearby).
Ordnance Survey

Trawlers in Grimsby docks. Lincolnshire Archives

Grimsby began to experience the same difficulties, but Otto Brand gave everyone a 'bad press' when he reported Papper as 'lost overboard' after a voyage, and then his senior crew began to tell the real story. The skipper had beaten the young man to death, just because the lad had made some remark about Brand having an affair with Papper's sister.

A few years before the end of the century, Mr Goodison, Secretary of the Fishermen's Federation, summed up what had been wrong with the system and why so much crime had developed. Goodison talked of 'the grasping, slave-driving trading propensities of the owners of the last twenty years or so', and said that boys had been rushed into the trade in a way reminiscent of slave-dealing. Nothing had changed, even by 1870, because 96 boys (around 10% of the total) had then been imprisoned. Historian Edward Gillett, writing in 1970, described the smugness of the owners at their sense of triumph in keeping the apprenticeship system going as they wanted it to be:

'. . . Alderman Mudd congratulated them [local magistrates] on their excellent administration of justice and noted that . . . . They had been able to preserve the apprenticeship system which in every other port was almost extinct.'

Maybe we get nearer to the truth of the wrongs of this system in the popular songs and ballads of the Victorian years, as in 'The Captain's Apprentice' of 1850:

*A boy to me was bound apprentice*
*Because his parents they were so poor;*
*I took him from St James's workhouse*
*All for to sail on some Spanish shore.*

*This boy one day he did offend me;*
*Well nothing to him did I say,*
*But straightway to the main shrouds I dragged him*
*And I kept him there till the very next day . . .*

The apprenticeship system survived until 1936.

# CHAPTER 16

# Tough Lives for Child Slaves
# c.1900

## You should remember that these boys are the scum of the earth . . .

In contrast to the factual account of prisons, runaways and masters, there is a documentary inquiry into the abuses of the system, and it comes most powerfully from one Robert Harborough Sherard in his book *The Child-Slaves of Britain,* published in the Edwardian period. Sherard came to Grimsby to find out the human experience behind the official reports and press desires for sensationalism. The book is generally written with a slight element of melodrama and Sherard has a tendency to overstate the case, but the fact is he came and interviewed people, including residents of the Fisher Lads' Institute, and of Burgess Street and King Edward Street.

Sherard was out to prove that in Grimsby there were despicable abuses of children going on and that there were law-breakers among the masters. He begins by saying that there is general cruelty and one of the first pieces of oral evidence is from an old seaman who says that he 'went through the mill like the rest of them, hung up by thumbs and all that . . .' But his first genuine talk with a knowledgeable local is merely a description of the system and seems neat and factual. But Sherard wants to paint things black. He writes about rumours of 'hazing and worse than that . . . practised on the fishing boats of the North Sea'. 'Hazing' is an old word for initiation tricks played on apprentices – as in all trades, something of a tradition. But he is implying that in Grimsby hazing was extreme.

What happens as Sherard gets closer to the professionals involved – such as the NSPCC staff – is that bias and callousness are found. He is told that there is no cruelty at all, that: 'You should remember that these boys are the scum of the earth.' But

# THE CHILD-SLAVES of BRITAIN

## By Robert Harborough Sherard

Author of " The White Slaves of England,"
" The Cry of the Poor,"
" At the Closed Door," etc.

*" Zwischen dem Ambos und Hammer."*—GOETHE.

London: Hurst and Blackett, Limited

182, High Holborn, W.C.   ❧   ❧   1905

Title page from Sherard's book. Author's collection

when faced with a charge of cruelty by the Southerner who has come to 'dig the dirt', one master says that hard labour is preferable to being sent over the water to Hull, and 'branded a gaol-bird to consort with thieves and to risk complete corruption'.

Then Sherard joins the ranks of those writers who lamented the lot of those who sank into prison sentences. One youth gives him a long and agonising account of being 'sent down'. Only through modern eyes does that seem like 'abuse'. So does Sherard find anything notably cruel? Eventually, he settles for finding the real horrors in homes, not on board ships. Sherard investigates the work of street-hawking and domestic labour and is revolted. The NSPCC man he meets describes no less than 177 cases of cruelty. A typical one is the tale of a fourteen-year-old boy who has been stuck in the back by a fork, thrown by his step-mother, and was punched regularly. Then, there is a boy of five who lights the house fire at six in the morning and labours all day – like a slave. The NSPCC inspector tells of children kept in filth, saying: '. . . bad heads are very common here – [with] vermin and sores'.

There is a crime, insists Sherard, that is committed by the magistrates, for they neglect all this and do nothing. In order to stress the need for change – if this state of affairs persists – we also hear about a murder story. An older man who has lived in this area of Hope Street has, reports Sherard, committed a murder, and was hanged in Lincoln Prison. He notes that: 'The prison chaplain said he had never met a more ignorant man.'

Finally, Sherard takes up the plight of homeless immigrants in the port, as well, describing the situation in these terms: 'The Emigrants' Home, on Grimsby Dock, must appear to many of the ragged wretches fleeing from their starvation holes in Poland, Russia and Croatia as the enchanted place of their hungry dreams . . .'

*The Child-Slaves of Britain* is one of a number of works at the end of the Victorian years in which the social investigators went into the poorest parts of the land in order to explore, much as Livingstone had done in Africa, the extent of crime, poverty and deprivation. Grimsby is depicted as the worst part of the land. Writers were indulging in their sources via police courts, shelters for the homeless and among the street urchins.

Sherard's book gives the reader several distortions but at least there is a genuine journey into the 'rabbit warrens' of the streets around the dock that were never really a presence in the official

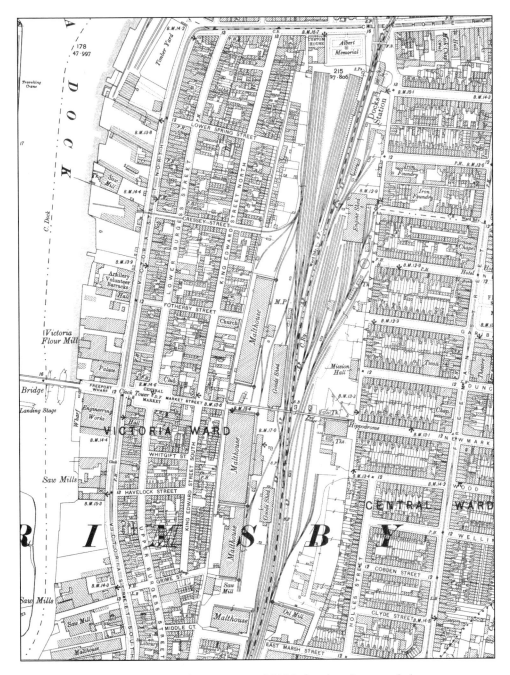

Large-scale Ordnance Survey map of 1906 showing the crowded streets around the docks. Ordnance Survey

reports of earlier decades. Sherard wants to say that the local officers of the law are the real criminals. Today, we can point to 'the system' and see in Grimsby at the time merely a reflection of the national situation regarding 'child slaves'. Nevertheless, Sherard has given an insight into the causes of crime beneath the larger picture of apprentice imprisonment and police work among the brothels and pubs at the time.

The verdict has to be that the crime he reports on is neglect.

# CHAPTER 17

# Lock-Out Trouble
# 1901

## . . . an outburst of angry rowdyism . . .

I n the last years of the nineteenth century, Grimsby suffered its own particular version of the social conflict of innovation versus the traditional way of working. In other words, the age of steam began to shift the centre of the economy. Money was being invested in the fishing industry on a larger scale and the ship owners obviously responded to the pressure to venture into trawlers, and so were set against the traditional smacks. By 1898, there were 277 smacks left to compete with 340 trawlers. Perhaps even more hurtful to the community sense of identity was the decline of share-fishing. What had always been a co-operative business run by shared profits from the catch now became a waged job. For some years there was a compromise when a percentage scheme was used, but the signs were there for all to see, that the future of fishing lay with waged men working for employers who would increasingly streamline the steam-powered trawlers.

The unity of the owners was ratified when their employers' group was formed, called the Grimsby Federated Owners Protection Society Ltd. That was a name whose very title implied a certain stance of defiance. A confrontation was likely after they insisted that the new regime would be the only one to operate. Grimsby was about to have its own Luddite resistance, amid the waves of new machines which were revolutionising not just the local economy but traditional ways of working. But there was a gradual increase in resentment as a stalemate continued and the year wore on. In October, the effects of the lock-out were felt. There were trawlers tied up and no crews. It was only a matter of time before blackleg labour would appear. First, the company of Smethurst tried to introduce foreign workers and the powder keg was lit. Rioting began, leading to the destruction of the Federation building. What followed was to lead to that familiar scenario in the English provinces when such events escalated. The troops were called in and the Riot Act was read in Riby Square.

The beginning of the trouble was when a huge crowd of around 4,000 people gathered around the Federation offices. As things turned nasty there were shouts of: 'We want Nesbitt' – the Secretary of the Federation. It was clear that a crew and engineers from Bradford had arrived. The rioting really took off then, and the crowd beat their way through the police line, followed by a burning hay-bale which was hurled into the building. Any thoughts of negotiation looked bleak after that, but there were attempts to calm things down.

It is fairly certain that there were outsiders in the crowd who were there to make sure that violence occurred and stones were thrown. This first act in the dispute, the attempt by the Excalibur Company to pay blacklegs, failed. One Bradford man even had the courage to stand and let the crowd know that he had come in ignorance of what the situation in Grimsby really was.

Something familiar to many towns happened then – as aldermen read the Riot Act they were booed and stoned. The

Temperance Hall, a key location in the riot. *The author*

town leaders, Doughty and Smethurst, had to be protected for the rest of the night. As with a similar riot in Lincoln ten years later, the usual events began to be put in place. There were more riots the next day and an increase in the forces of authority called were drafted. There was a massive gathering of people in the market place and there were rough fights with the police when more officers arrived. The Police Watch Committee were trying to decide on just how much help they needed and, finally, it was ordered that army detachments should come, along with twenty-five mounted police.

Later in the second day of the troubles, the worst reprisal happened, something that anyone with a sense of history at the time would have dreaded. The imported Sheffield police charged the crowd with batons. There were children and young people present but that situation was ignored by the police. The attack was heartlessly brutal. Many people were sent to hospital but nothing changed the attitude of the police, who charged again at the crowd assembled by the Temperance Hall. There were fires and more simmering resentment. Anything could have happened by way of a vendetta, such was the mood of the crowd. A measure of the scale of the fighting was that three gun boats arrived in the Humber – surely something that was totally un-necessary – and this gave a clear indication of the lack of any consideration for human life within the powers of authority, even from the Home Office.

Trying to imagine the strained situation of peace at that weekend is very difficult. Townspeople were walking around among police officers who a few days before had set about them mercilessly with batons and troops stood on guard on street corners. It was a time of repression, when all kinds of announce-ments were made threatening dire consequences to any 'subversive' action. There were accounts in the papers of atrocities, including one tale of a plain clothes police officer who had been attacked with a brick. On a national level, *The Times* reported that: 'We have pointed out to both that the prolongation of the struggle, unless it is supported by those who command large resources, is certain to end in defeat.' But the *Sheffield Independent* saw things as: '. . . an outburst of angry rowdyism for which the fishermen who are unemployed cannot be held responsible.'

One thing is certain: before any kind of compromise was reached, the police actions were the most reprehensible element in the riots. Their actions had been unpardonable. Over 600

A sailing smack in Grimsby docks. Lincolnshire Archives

officers had had to be fed and bedded in various locations and the estimated cost was £300 a day. As was always the case in such major riots, a period of recriminations followed, then an attempt to sort out grievances with an eye of the sullenness of defeat. A meeting at the Prince of Wales Theatre in the presence of Lord Yarborough was the first step in a process moving towards a settlement. Once the issue of men signing on at the Board of Trade was settled, an end to trouble was in sight.

Sir Edward Fry was the independent arbiter and he and his committee spelled out the conditions on which peace was signed – as if a war was over – and to some extent the feeling must have been one of having survived a military conflict. The main points stated were that 'signing on' would be related to conditions of work and wages; and poundage would be settled individually. Employers were not confined to recruiting union labour.

The whole episode was typical of every lock-out during the long Industrial Revolution in Britain. In an organisational sense it had the features of police panic and overreaction, but on an individual, human level, it had entailed a baton charge in which

Steam trawlers laid up during the strike. Lincolnshire Archives

women and children had been crushed or beaten. Generations of Grimsby people would never forget this assault and the resentment rankled for decades.

A lock-out excludes more than workers – it also locks out trust and respect – and the event in Grimsby, in 1901, proves that. It was a terrible start to the new century. In many ways, a community has to cope with mental scars that linger on for a very long time. With hindsight, we can see that the causes of the problems in Grimsby could have been so easily avoided by those in power.

# Chapter 18

# A Murdering Mariner
# 1903

## Lucy had been stabbed eleven times – in the head, face, chest and arms . . .

amuel Smith and Lucy Lingard were both very drunk on 18 November 1902. Smith was forty-five and Lucy thirty-three. They both lived away from their spouses. Smith tended to live in with Lucy and her four children, whenever he happened to be home from the sea. He was a Devonian sailor who had befriended Lucy and her husband and he used to drop in and eat with them from time to time. When Lucy left her husband, Sam Smith was her closest friend, so they grew close.

Sam and Lucy moved into Fourth Terrace, Hope Street, and life should have been brighter for Lucy, but Sam was a man with a bad temper and he could be very unstable. On a black day in November, they had been on a drinking binge all afternoon and, when they returned home, took a quart of ale with them – not a smart move when we recall that they had been arguing for hours, and there was a rage simmering in Sam Smith. Lucy's eldest daughter, Rose, was in the room when Smith began to lose control. He hit Rose in the face and gave her a black eye. Lucy decided to go to bed and leave him to brood.

At that point, two neighbours, both women, called Martin and Summerfield, came to talk to her. They seem to have been aware of the trouble and, of course, the black eye was the focus of their conversation. The women were very supportive and took it on themselves to give Samuel Smith a ticking off for doing such an awful thing to Rose. Smith did manage to apologise, so all must have seemed well to them when they left the couple and Rose in the house.

The two women had left late, at around eleven at night, but not long after they heard a scream. Someone else from the street,

The old Victorian prison, Lincoln, used for the apprentice lads and others.
The author

a Mrs Ward, was quickly on the scene and there she saw Smith standing over his Lucy's body, moving to a chair when Ward arrived. Rose had also raised the alarm, racing out into the street to shout for a policeman. It was clear that Lucy had tried in vain to protect herself but she was savagely wounded, having been stabbed eleven times – in the head, face, chest and arms. She died in hospital four days later. It transpired that Samuel Smith had seen that she was in agony when he stepped away from her, then took up the knife again and renewed the attack.

There was a feeling in some quarters that if both were drunk, then blame might be hard to apportion, particularly as it was a common opinion that Smith was 'feeble-minded' – but he had killed her brutally and the verdict of wilful murder would not be difficult to arrive at. When Sam Smith was sentenced to death the townsfolk began to take more interest in the crime and a petition was raised. It was destined to be a futile act, however.

Smith is on record of having said that the woman was not at all to blame and that there had been nothing to provoke him on her part. He had killed her in a rage and thrown the knife into the fireplace. Mr Justice Kennedy, at Lincoln Assizes, had no alternative but to sentence Samuel Smith to be hanged. He was a client of hangman William Billington and left this life at Lincoln Prison, on 10 March 1903.

Throughout the Victorian period, there had been repeated attempts to make out that intoxication might well be categorised as a defence in murder trials, but the very best lawyers in the land had failed to give this any substance – so there was no point in Smith's defence, led by Mr Binner, even contemplating such a thing. Vague, half-baked lines of thought about his 'feeble-mindedness' also never materialised into any kind of justification. To local people the case would be labelled a fight between two drunks – a very common occurrence around Hope Street at the time. But there is no doubt that poor Lucy carried no blame at all for the terrible way she had her life taken from her.

# CHAPTER 19

# Capture of a Spy
# 1915

## Some of his friends were with big German liners laid up at Rotterdam

I n the years before the Great War England was subject to fits of spy mania. People were seeing German spies everywhere and anyone with a German name was open to suspicion. The newspapers were full of lurid accounts of supposed spies on trial. Even the writer D H Lawrence, who had married a German, and was living in Cornwall, was thought to be involved in sending signals to German submarines – though nothing was ever proved.

In this atmosphere, Grimsby had its episode of spy activity. A Swede called Ernst Olsson was convicted at Lincoln Assizes on 17 June 1915 of trying to gather information that would constitute an offence under the Official Secrets Act of 1911. The Act and all its provisions sprang from years of uncertainty about how to change and streamline the military intelligence of the realm. After the Boer War (1899–1902) and the dynamic growth of the German Empire in Africa, Britain was confused about how to plan and improve its actions against espionage at home. The German intelligence system, initially naval, with Admiral von Tirpitz in charge, was certainly organising a spy ring here, and the new MI5 department under Colonel Vernon Kell, had been impressively effective against these spies who were looking for information at dockyards.

Every seaport was vulnerable and Grimsby was no exception. Olsson was charged with looking for information about the defences and sea power elements as observed in the Humber. Another Swede who was living in Grimsby, called Erander, had been working with him. On 16 March a conversation between the two had been overheard and reported. In this interchange they said that in the coming war the Germans were sure to win.

Olsson talked about some German friends in Rotterdam, saying that they were trying to extract some information about the naval and military situation in Grimsby. He was heard asking Erander for that type of information. The two men were being tailed and clearly it was not difficult to listen in on their talk, because a week later they were listened to again and this time Erander was asked if he had made a decision about passing on such information. Erander's actual words were noted. He said: 'Life is sweeter than money to me; I have been in Grimsby fifteen years and I have been treated like a man, and it would be the last thing I should do.'

That second conversation was the foundation of the accusation against Olsson. He had said that some of his friends were Germans with big German liners laid up at Rotterdam. On 7 April they met again and he repeated that statement. Olsson said that his friends over the North Sea were working hard to obtain

The fate of a German spy - from the British Magazine. Author's collection

the military information. Then, stepping up the talk to something more definite and alarming, he spoke of a fleet of 130 or 170 Zeppelins that were ready to fly over the sea to drop bombs on England when the weather was right. When the talkative Swede actually moved on to talk about his being a U-Boat pilot he was really in trouble. After that, Olsson wandered into *Boy's Own* territory, with a discourse about him being set up in a small boat on the East Coast 'with petrol and provisions to supply the Germans at sea'.

Lipson Ward, defending the Swede, managed to argue that last statement away, defining it as 'irrelevant' to the charge. At his appeal hearing in February, the last statement was successfully removed as indictable, but the second ground for appeal – that the trial had been prejudiced by a card found on his person – was judged to be admissible. The card had been a summary of naval signalling, something that it was argued was generally available and he had owned it since 1911.

The judge, Mr Justice Horridge, allowed the charge about the card to stand and the Swede was cross-examined. Everything the defence could come up with failed, so Olsson was sentenced to four years' penal servitude. The Official Secrets Act, something people were still trying to fully understand, had clearly laid down that penal servitude was the punishment for 'communicating or intending to communicate secrets to a foreign state or an agent of a foreign state'. Olsson's talk of 'friends in Rotterdam' had been his downfall.

In the same year, a certain Carl Muller had been executed by firing squad for spying. Muller also had friends in Rotterdam and he had sent letters to them written in German, about shipping dispositions. Robert Rosenthal met the same fate after sending coded details to Germany about shipping in Hull.

The efficiency of the team of officers led by Kell in London was astonishing. It stemmed from an overheard conversation on a train in which two Germans were discussing a letter from Potsdam about British preparations for war. Grimsby played its part in that successful counter-espionage ring and the detectives, busy at the port, were part of a team working at all major ports. As far as Olsson was concerned, there seems to have been an element of fantasy and wish-fulfilment in his ramblings to his friend. In fact, the words spoken by his friend are very important in understanding the depth of support for counter-espionage among civilians. After all, Erander had been welcomed and respected in his adopted country and this was a buffer against the blandishments of his friend, who was convinced of German superiority.

As a writer to the paper had said in the same year, when discussing the German spy scares: 'Altogether different is the position of the spy in time of peace. In some cases he is merely an adventurer working for money; he is then corrupt and it is his business to corrupt others . . .' That is exactly what Olsson was trying to do, but he was too bold and careless. He would never have made a James Bond. But there was a larger scale development well into operation. The spymasters in Germany *had* organised a widespread operation. In 1907, a man called Widenmann had taken over as naval attaché in England, and he had three agents ready and waiting to serve him.

One of these agents, de Boer, managed to start an association linking his work with the Argo Steamship Company, based in Bremen. De Boer would act as the agent in Hull and Grimsby, working for the organisation in Germany running espionage, known as the *Admiralstab*. The plan didn't really work and de Boer was neglected by his masters for some time.

But what this does tell us is that characters like Olsson were around the ports, ready and willing to be approached and enlisted by men like de Boer? We have to wonder whether, on a day when Olsson was hanging around and up to no good, he met either de Boer or one of his cronies. Certainly something fired him with enthusiasm for Germany and its imperial designs. Still, thanks to the beginnings of MI5 in the establishment of the Secret Service under Captain Vernon Kell in 1909, the German spy ring never succeeded; but that did not stop spy scares such as this one in Grimsby. However, it did make the men involved in them easier to track down. Methods of reconnaissance were so sophisticated by 1911 that it was almost impossible for an amateur like Olsson to achieve anything – and, with his lack of tact and tendency to brag, he was doomed to failure from the start. By the last phase of pre-war activities by aspiring German spies, one of their leaders wrote that: 'For the time being the matter [of spying] works on no account.' That never stopped the irrational stories of Germans hiding in cupboards, and the terrible destruction of property owned by anyone with a German-sounding name still happened regularly in the war years.

# CHAPTER 20

# Cruelty to an Objector
# Cleethorpes, 1917

**I'll make it so damned uncomfortable for you,
that you will be glad to start soldiering for
your own protection . . .**

During the First World War, as we now understand so well, it took astounding courage not to sign up as a 'Tommy' and go across to fight on the Western Front. The fate of conscientious objectors was sometimes desperately sad and entailed humiliation and imprisonment. But, at times, their treatment plumbed the depths of inhumanity, and historians today have to ask who was really doing a criminal act – the victim or the regime at the time? Strictly according to law, the objector was to be imprisoned – but that did not mean that the person should then be treated like scum, dehumanised and tortured. This was the fate of one young man in Cleethorpes.

James Brightmore was from Manchester. He found himself in the Council House at Cleethorpes in July 1917, for refusing to obey an order. He had already suffered such ignominy that his case had reached parliament and 'some officers involved had retired'. In June of that year, he had refused to assemble his equipment and witnesses from the army had testified to that effect. He argued that the order was illegal and indeed 'unusual'.

Earlier that year, he had been sentenced to nine months in Lincoln Prison (reduced to six later) for an offence 'committed as a conscientious objector'. From that point there had been a campaign against him, lasting from the January up to his appearance in July. First, he was asked to pick up waste paper and refused. He was then given twenty-three days' solitary confinement and his officer said to him: 'I'll make it so damned uncomfortable for you, that you will be glad to start soldiering for your own protection.' A reign of terror began.

His tormentor, Captain McBean, said: 'Give him [James

Brightmore] Devonport rations and let him cook them himself. Put him among the Expeditionary Force men but don't let him mix with them. He isn't fit to associate with soldiers. Cut his buttons and badges off . . . he is a disgrace to them.' It is not clear whether the officer meant by 'Devonport rations', that the man should be tied up, or whether he simply meant meagre food, as implied by the old myth about 'Devon's share', meaning the very worst leftovers. But whatever his meaning, a terrible and hateful regime of punishment began against Brightmore.

Brightmore was taken to a hole which had been dug to a depth of four feet and he was left to stand there. Later, it was deepened to seven feet. He was left in the hole and refused any food. The next day the hole was deepened and Brightmore continued to remain there; and he was soon standing in water. Brightmore's account was as follows:

> *I spent most of the day in the hole, water accumulating until it was ankle-deep. I refused food that day. Next morning, June 30, they came and took another two feet of mud and clay out of the hole. I found my strength failing and ate some bread and margarine. It rained and I was wet through but at night a corporal let me out and let me sleep in a marquee . . .*

The corporal was severely reprimanded for his act of humanity. But the punishment continued, even to the point of the officer providing a piece of wood for the victim to stand on: a pathetic attempt to limit the suffering, but it was of no help. Then Brightmore was hauled before a medical officer.

By that time he was becoming more determined to take on his tormentor and be uncooperative whenever he could, so he refused the medical inspection. The officer did not enforce the examination, so the doctor merely looked at the prisoner and said he looked fit – and he was passed fit. Again, after eating some beans and meat, another day passed in the hole. One man let him go to the marquee but he was sent back to the hole. Brightmore was left in the water, at the bottom of the hole, for another four days, in the bitter east wind. He said: 'During Thursday night I dozed a bit, but my limbs ached so that I could not sleep. I was in a state of collapse by morning, and asked to see a doctor.'

It is amazing to read that Brightmore was then taken before a senior officer, still in his soaking clothes. He was asked if he had any cause for complaints and he chose that moment to go through the awful treatment he had received. The only effect that this had was that he was taken to the guard tent rather than the hole, still in his wet clothes.

The real bone of contention – that Brightmore insisted that a conscientious objector should not be treated as a soldier – escalated the situation when McBean asked to see him and told him that he would be treated as a soldier. At that interview, the poor man had been in the hole for eleven days. It was not long afterwards that he refused to assemble his equipment, not defining himself as 'a soldier'. As Brightmore stood in court, in July, he repeated that he could not be punished for a military offence, since he was not a soldier.

McBean had become seriously ill by that time, and he came to the inquiry from his sick bed in Leeds. Brightmore had known about this and had asked for an adjournment so that his torturer could attend. It was clearly a case of a battle of wills and a sense of deep injustice. The military hearing could not decide on a course of action and the case dragged on. It had to end in an impasse and so it did, being deferred with no decision. In the end, the only course of action was to remove McBean from the situation, and that resolved matters. But the story is one of the worst cases of cruelty against a conscientious objector in those terrible years when to be given 'the white feather' was a disgrace, and when intellectuals and activists were imprisoned for their political views. Brightmore must have been longing to be home in Manchester, where he probably would have preferred a stretch in Strangeways to any more time with McBean in Cleethorpes.

# Chapter 21

# Poor Law Guardian Murdered 1919

## She was a good woman, robbed of her life while caring for the needy

I n November 1919, a group of outstanding and influential people wrote a joint letter to *The Times* on the subject of the 'feeble-minded' in society. Those who signed included the Chief Rabbi and also Cardinal Bourne, and politicians of note including George Lansbury and Henry Hobhouse. They wrote about the limitations of the new Mental Deficiency Act which had come into force in 1913, and their main concerns were about what was going to happen to those people with severe mental illness in the workhouses:

*We wish to emphasise the moral aspect of the question. There is every indication that this branch of the subject needs careful study . . . The evidence so far is conclusive that a feeble-minded person is more easily swayed by vicious influences than a normal person and that mentally defective boys or girls when Thrown into bad company are easy prey to immoral and criminal tendencies . . .*

The dignitaries had good cause to worry about such things. Just four months before their letter was published, Mrs Mary Robinson, a Poor Law Guardian, from Cleethorpes, was killed by Joseph Woodhall. Woodhall was found to be insane at court in Lincoln, and therefore sentenced to be detained 'during His Majesty's pleasure'. The Guardian was a good woman, robbed of her life while caring for the needy.

Workhouses were intended, as the 'mission statement' of a Norfolk institution proclaimed: 'For the instruction of youth, the encouragement of industry, the relief of want, the support of old age and the comfort of infirmity and pain.' But they also had to cater for the mentally disturbed, from schizophrenics to bi-polar depressives.

There had been concern about female staff in workhouses ever since women began to be allowed to work in such places in the 1880s. In fact, just before the new Act was passed there had been a statement made in 1912 by the Chairman of the National Association of the Feeble-Minded, William Chance, to the effect that there were around 20% feeble-minded people in

The workhouse, Scartho Road. Author's collection

the workhouses and that these conditions were likely to be a particular problem for female guardians who might be faced with 'a need to physically restrain certain inmates when under duress'. How right he was. Chance had pointed out that the workhouses had large numbers of people who could be classified as 'thieves, prostitutes, paupers, inebriates, lunatics and feeble-minded'. Chance desperately wanted to see 'better protection and control' of people with mental problems in confinement and he was onto something very important, and it was a subject not fully tackled in the new legislation.

There had been terrible problems in the workhouses for many decades and, since the sensational affair of the cruelty at Andover workhouse in 1846, the Government had tried to improve conditions for inmates. In a society experiencing the accelerated social change of the Industrial Revolution, there were large numbers of casualties as people could not cope after losing jobs and loved ones. By 1870, one third of the population of England was living in a workhouse of some kind.

In Grimsby, there had been an early workhouse, called a 'House of Industry' since 1834 when the New Poor Law came into practice. Grimsby was included in the area covered by the Caistor Poor Law Union. By the end of the century, however, the new workhouse in Scartho Road had been built, opened in 1894 by the Rt Hon J Shaw-Le-Fevre. There were separate blocks for the various types of inmate, as the large-scale Ordnance Survey map for 1906 shows. So-called 'imbeciles' were housed on the eastern side of the site. But of course 'imbeciles' and the 'feeble-minded' were blanket terms for all kinds of mental illness, from eccentricity to sheer psychopathic natures. For instance, the 'Laceby Hermit', Bobby Marples, spent time in the workhouse after his hut on the Laceby to Aylesby Road was burnt down. Of course, Bobby's case is merely one extreme example. He was not a homicidal maniac. Unfortunately, Mary Robinson did meet one such type that fateful day in July 1919.

A man who would have been included in that group often called the 'despair and reproach of the criminal law' was in Scartho Road when Mrs Robinson was going about her work. With hindsight, it is hard to believe how vulnerable workhouse staff were in these situations. Under the various Lunacy Acts staff were still locked in with lunatic inmates until a decision was reached as to whether they merited a transfer to the massive asylum at Bracebridge, south of Lincoln. The supposed lunatics

COMMITTEE ON INSANITY AND CRIME,

# REPORT

OF THE

Committee appointed to consider what changes, if any, are
desirable in the existing law, practice and procedure
relating to criminal trials in which the plea of insanity
as a defence is raised, and whether any and, if so,
what changes should be made in the existing
law and practice in respect of cases falling
within the provisions of section 2 (4)
of the Criminal Lunatics Act, 1884,

*Presented to Parliament by Command of His Majesty.*

LONDON:

PRINTED & PUBLISHED BY HIS MAJESTY'S STATIONERY OFFICE.

To be purchased directly from H.M. STATIONERY OFFICE at the following addresses:
Imperial House, Kingsway, London, W.C.2; 28, Abingdon Street, London, S.W.1;
York Street, Manchester; 1, St. Andrew's Crescent, Cardiff;
or 120, George Street, Edinburgh;
or through any Bookseller.

1924

Price 6d. net.

Report on Insanity and Crime, 1924. Author's collection

would be in the workhouse on a fourteen-day order until a decision was made.

The vulnerability of those good people staffing the work-houses went on for some considerable time. Mrs Robinson was one of the unluckiest ones.

# CHAPTER 22

# Cruelty in the Village
# 1919

## Lower down on the same leg was a bruise measuring five inches . . .

I n the twenty-first century, we fret about what degree of physical punishment might be given to a recalcitrant child. We worry about what constitutes a slap or what is a mild as opposed to a heavy punishment, and about what a parent should be aware of in that context. There were no such worries a century ago, as physical punishment was common practice. As late as the 1950s, schoolteachers were administering quite severe punishment with canes in our schools and pupils were sometimes even struck about the head. But even around the turn of the nineteenth century, there were limits.

Inspector Francis, an officer for the NSPCC in Grimsby, found himself being called out into the country to the village of Wootton, in April 1919. He had a complaint of cruelty on the part of a platelayer called Arthur Edwards on his son, Reginald. It was an unpleasant business, and was to involve the police, and destined to appear as a case in the courtroom.

At Barton Police Court Edwards stood accused of extreme cruelty, faced by Chapman, the Grimsby lawyer working for the NSPCC. Chapman had plenty of disturbing and ugly evidence. Edwards said that he had taken the boy to his brother's place in Grantham because he could not control him. He said: 'I have beaten the boy but he's not here.' Pathetically, the accused thought that he could play for time, hoping evidence would not be apparent if time went on. But Sergeant Hallam had interviewed him and then, after the victim had been seen at Grantham, there was a report. Hallam stated that he was satisfied that Edwards had 'beaten the boy unnecessarily and unmercifully'. For merely mixing chicken food, the accused said, he had beaten the boy with a cane.

Hallam and the inspector found a large black bruise on the back of the boy's leg measuring five inches by one and another, five inches by three. Both bruises were tender. The officer said: 'Both bruises were not such as would be caused by reasonable castigation.' There was a long history to the regime of punishment, however. He had lived away from Edwards for three years and had been accused of petty theft. But there had always been extreme punishments given to the boy. He had been locked in a washhouse and given a diet of bread and water after refusing to do some chores set for him.

On one occasion the boy was late home from school and, as a result, according to the inspector: 'Edwards took him into the washhouse and proceeded to thrash him with a cane and afterwards with a thick stick used for mixing chicken food.' Reginald was severely injured and squealed in pain. He was so aggrieved that he went the next day to tell a neighbour of his ill treatment, a farmer called Clifford Kendall. He told Kendall that he had been thrashed with a belt at times before the current attack, and that certainly had an effect. Kendall told the court that the boy had shown him bruises on the back of his leg, and that these were black. The farmer said: 'I've been interested in watching the boy because I always felt sure that he was being knocked about.'

As for Edwards, when he made his statement in defence of his actions he said that Reginald was 'a very bad boy, very dirty in his bedroom, generally late home from school'. He argued that before the events of April when Kendall had been involved, he had only 'cautioned' the boy. He explained that on the day in question he had simply asked the boy why he had not done as he was told and brought in sticks and coal? Edwards was clearly irritated by all kinds of small offences, referring to Reginald's tearing clothes while bird watching and being rude to his grandmother. But Edwards claimed that he never lost his temper and had not used the big stick on the child.

Reginald had obviously received treatment well out of all correlation to his petty annoyances and the NSPCC won the day. Edwards was ordered to pay a £3 fine and £3.10s in costs. That was hardly a deterrent and, of course, the victim had not been removed from the company of his tormentor. We have to wonder what happened back at the family house. Protection was limited then, and the inspector in Grimsby, along with the police sergeant, surely realised that they could easily find themselves repeating that awful experience. Edwards was capable of doing even worse things, such was his cruel streak. We have no record of further offences, but that does not mean that the nasty piece of work in Wootton was restrained or that he changed in any way.

# CHAPTER 23

# The Jockey Con Man
# 1919

## The prisoner got the better of a struggle with her . . .

Cleethorpes, along with most other holiday places after the Great War, was a location in which all kinds of rogues were looking for easy money. The years immediately after the 1918 Armistice were in many ways terrible times. There was extreme hardship everywhere and widespread unemployment. Crime statistics of the time show a high rise in fraudsters and con men. Their victims were usually weak and vulnerable or, as in this case, young and impressionable.

The victim was young Edith May Ambler of Tiverton Street. She had an encounter with a rogue from Spilsby called Thomas Charles Jones. They met near the pier in August and he impressed Edith, taking her to play golf and spinning yarns. He said he was a jockey and showed her a business card saying: 'G Jones, Jockey, Leicester Square.' She was taken in and he began his campaign on her gullibility. First, he stole her wristwatch and then led her into crime in her own town.

Things became more serious. As the newspaper reported at the time, 'The prisoner got the better of a struggle with her . . . and they had immoral relations.' In other words, Edith was raped. But she kept company with him still, and although he claimed that he was going to be on the move and heading for Nottingham, he appears to have stayed at the *Royal Hotel* in Grimsby and then when they met again, he had a new watch, bragging that it was particularly expensive. He put the watch on her wrist and continued his wooing. But it was stolen and he was tracked down by police.

In court, Jones insisted that the new watch had been bought in London and that he had never seen the watch previously owned by the hapless Edith. Questioning turned to the supposed profession of jockey that Jones had claimed. Superintendent Sindall asked how long it was since the accused had ridden in a race, and he replied vaguely that it had been the April of that year, and at Warwick.

The truth began to emerge under questioning: the fact was that Jones existed as a gambler and adventurer looking for easy prey. As the reporter put in large print at the time, he 'LIVED BY HIS WITS'. Clearly, these were malevolent wits. When he was asked what his profession was other than being a jockey, he said: 'I back horses.' Jones had apparently been married and questioning turned to that subject as the prosecution tried to worm out the truth about this charlatan:

> *Are you married?*
> *Yes.*
> *Where is your wife?*
> *She left me.*

He was then asked if he knew an Ella Pettit and if so, was she respectable? It was all to ascertain that he had been living with that woman while on the move, committing similar crimes for which he was wanted, in Worcester and in Wales. The only shred of truth about his supposedly being a jockey was that he had had a licence when he left school but there was no evidence that he had ever ridden professionally.

Despite the claim that there was no hard evidence against Jones, he was sentenced to six months' hard labour. The magistrates, Brockway and Major Bennett, believed what the witnesses had said. The crook's antics had actually involved young Edith in a theft, as the watch and other property belonged to William Parsons, of Queen's Parade in Cleethorpes. Wisely, Superintendent Sindall did not proceed with any action against the two young people together for that second count. It would have been cruel in the extreme to do so, as poor Edith had suffered humiliation enough.

The sad case became just one more statistic in those hard times. We have no knowledge of whether or not prison did anything to change Jones – it seems unlikely.

# CHAPTER 24

# Wages Gone Astray
# 1922

## The jury were told not to listen to the lame story of the mystery man in the dock . . .

ometimes in the history of crime, a man's good name and reputation count for very little. That certainly applied to the case of an ex-army officer who had a position of trust in Grimsby.

Lieutenant Walter Masterman stood in the dock at Lincoln Assizes in July 1922, to answer charges of fraud. He was district Sea Fisheries Officer in Grimsby, employed by the Board of Agriculture and Fisheries. As he was a military man and a person of high social status, it was a case that would set tongues wagging in his home town. But forty-five-year-old Masterman would prove to be a complex personality as the trial went on.

In legal language, he had 'forged and uttered a receipt for monies', which in plain English means that he committed fraud by means of a simple forgery while in a position of trust. Between 1920 and late 1921, he had made almost £1,000 by these means. Hugo Young, leading the prosecution, told the jury that Masterman had been in the habit of also forging names of illiterate employees, as in one instance when the paymaster had actually forged the cross by the name of one Mr Larken. The same act was done several times for other men.

There was a case for the defence, and it was calculated to create a certain amount of sympathy for the defendant; he was supposedly suffering from bad health and that, in the period when the cheques were alleged to have been forged, Masterman was in fact in a nursing home. He had been at that time, the lawyer said, 'hard pressed for money and his bankers were writing to him demanding settlement . . .'

Typists and payments clerks gave evidence regarding the supposed wages fraud. It was noted that the junior employees were in the habit of taking wages slips to Masterman or to another clerk when the employees did not turn up to collect wages. It was shown that Larken, for example, had been in Hull on the day his mark was forged. The truth began to come through when Larken himself appeared and made a statement to the effect that he had never worked at the place. He added: 'I never gave anybody any authority to receive money for me, and at the time of all this, I was out at sea, fishing.'

It was considered by the defence, that the court should hear something of Masterman's army record. The Chief Inspector of Fisheries, Mr M Blundell, took on this duty. After hearing that Masterman had perhaps invented an employee named Hart, and that there never was a Hart in the Fisheries Department, Blundell had a tough task ahead of him. Three men who had been employed working on ex-German trawlers were asked about 'Hart' and shook their heads.

Blundell gave a summary, but then Masterman intervened and pointed out that he had contracted enteric fever while serving in the Boer War in 1901. Laying it on thick, he also described his suffering from trench fever in the Great War, fresh in everyone's mind of course. Masterman noted that adapting to life in a situation in which those who had previously taken orders from him and were now his equals, was hard. That did not gather much sympathy from those listening.

The defence kept retelling the tale of the visit by the mysterious 'Larken' and this drove Hugo Young into a more aggressive tone of questioning, shouting: 'Why presume that this mystery man's name was Larken?'

'Because his was the only name on the sheet,' replied Masterman. 'I always called him Larken to his face.' Young turned to the jury and decided to give them a lecture: he said:

*Do not listen to the lame story of the mystery man in the dock . . .*

Responding, the defence lawyer rather desperately asked a rhetorical question: 'Can the jury accept the evidence of a man's word in spite of the evidence against him?' The defence also added that Masterman's army record, stretching from 1900 to 1920 was 'unimpeachable'. But the jury took a mere twenty-five minutes to find Masterman guilty of forgery but recommended mercy. He must have been relieved to hear that other indictments were not proceeded with.

Masterman bowed to the judge when His Lordship made his

remarks about the pity of an honourable name being ruined, and when the sentence of three years' penal servitude was given. Perhaps wanting to hint at his clemency to the jury, the judge pointed out that the maximum sentence tariff for penal servitude was fourteen years.

As for Masterman, he probably had some comfort in seeing that *The Times* devoted only one meagre paragraph to the crime and sentence. The report summed up his actions perfectly: 'He was not charged with paying to a wrong man, but not paying at all.'

# CHAPTER 25

# Car Crime Wave
# 1937

## Hutson was killed, his head striking a
## telegraph pole

ooking at past years in the history of Grimsby for those years in which it could be said that people were living dangerously, a strong case can be made for 1937. It was a year in which there were frightening frequent mishaps, collisions and road deaths on all sides. In one case, even a police officer was guilty, and in another, a seventy-year-old killed a man. The *Grimsby News* carried adverts for the pleasures of the 'motor charabanc' but many surely trembled at the thought. The roads were indeed places of maiming and death, and speeds were not at all high by today's standards.

A police officer, just three days after taking his test, smashed his car into a girl cyclist in Cleethorpes; his driving 'without due care and attention' led to his driving his vehicle into the cyclist Jean Carter, near the *Imperial Hotel* in Grimsby Road. There were plenty of witnesses of course, and it was an entertaining story that one of the 'men in blue' stood in the dock for a change. The officer was doing the horribly high speed of *four miles an hour* when he turned into Blundell Avenue. We might laugh today, but the fact is that the cyclist was thrown several yards from her cycle and was fortunate not to be seriously hurt.

Then there was the farmer from Holton-le-Clay who was fined over £3 for reckless driving on the Waltham to Louth Road. The farmer caused another car to swerve and plunge into a ditch. The defendant claimed that there was plenty of room for the other man to pass, but the statement did him no good. The fact was that the farmer had previous convictions for driving without due care. Section 78 of the Highway Act of 1835 had the man guilty as well: 'If the driver of any wagon, cart or other carriage . . . shall not keep to the left or near side of the road . . .' etc.

# EDUCATING ROAD USERS

'Educating Road Users', 1937. *The Times*

---

## 800 MORE MOBILE POLICE

Sir John Simon, the Home Secretary, announced in the House of Commons yesterday that it is proposed, as an experiment, to augment the number of police road patrols by about 800 men, not so much with a view to more frequent penal action, but primarily for the purpose of inculcating a higher standard of road sense and behaviour on the part of all classes of road users, including cyclists and pedestrians.

It is understood (our Parliamentary Correspondent writes) that the new scheme will begin in two experimental areas, one in the North of England and the other in the South. The police to be employed will be specially trained, and it may be possible to make use of the special training facilities available for the Metropolitan Police at Hendon. For the experimental period it is proposed to quadruple the present motor patrol strength in the areas selected. The scheme cannot be put into operation until recruits have been appointed and trained to take

More seriously, in some crimes there was death and carnage. Consider Mr Cross, a retired accountant. Cross drove his motor car while under the influence of drink and was fortunate indeed not to face a charge of manslaughter, as he caused the death of Eric Hutson at Holton-le-Clay. Hutson was killed, his head striking a telegraph pole. From one point of view, Cross's rashness was easy to defend, because, as his defence stated, 'Cross was not addicted to drink and he would undertake not to drive again.' He was ordered to pay £100 costs and disqualified from holding a driving licence for the rest of his life. Cross had a hard man in the judge's seat – no less a figure than the famous Mr Justice Travers Humphreys.

The Superintendent of Police's report, in February 1937, stated that there had been twelve convictions for 'driving under the influence' in the past three years; so 1937 was a real acceleration in the offence. Just one week after the report, a cyclist in Louth was killed by a reckless driver. Young Percy Hewson was on his bike when a car came at him at speed, and with its lights out; that was at half past ten on a Saturday night. The unfortunate doctor called to the scene said that death was instantaneous.

Grimsby folk must have been walking into the streets with their hearts thumping in dire anticipation of a vehicle aiming at crushing them or knocking them across the road. Clearly, something needed to be done on the driving tests, and the evidence was gathering that driving offences were going to be a feature of future crime. Bert Fryer, the central figure in the next chapter, started work on his beat in Cleethorpes in this very year. He was

## ES NOTES.

leethorpes Nursing
s of the Cleethorpes
Society gave a num-
ays at St. Peter's
esday and Wednes-
rogramme included
" (Wendy St. John
players were Myra
les, Margaret Rey-
an, Margaret Croft
e and Gladys Earl
ducer was Marjorie
Without Men." by
was presented by
Edith Bower. Pearl
iers, Kathleen Dale,
Ruby Smith, with C.
er. "The Flaw," by
i is the play which
ered in the British
n competition, was
e Meller, and the
Beckitt, I. Rosen-
d, Florence Ryder,
arrison and A. B.
umber on the pro-
eer Street " (John
uich E. M. Mawson, W.
Eileen Mawson, W.
nan and W. Garner
produced by Ada

ried out the duties
W. Garner was the
Ida Nocton as the
nager. Furniture
loaned by Mr. H.
al music was pro-
uttor's trio.

—

ure.

Salvation Army in
up with work in
subject of an
ven at the Clee-
my headquarters,
r, by Lieut.-Com-
isidering the time
was held, there
e present, under
he Deputy Mayor
councillor Jesse
pported by some

---

## POLICE OFFICER FINED.

## Driving Offence at Cleethorpes.

### COLLISION THREE DAYS AFTER TEST.

As the result of a collision between
his motor car and a girl cyclist at
Cleethorpes on 2nd January, a police
constable, Thomas Webster Richardson,
of Great Coates, appeared at the
Grimsby County Police Court, on Tuesday, charged with driving a motor car
without due care and attention.

Mr. H. S. Bloomer appeared for the
defendant and entered a plea of not
guilty.

After outlining the details of the case,
Supt. Brumfield said the whole of the
facts had been submitted to , is . } ief
Constable.

" He has instructed me to proceed
with the case, and place the facts before
your Worships and leave you to
decide," he said.

#### CYCLIST'S STORY.

According to Jean Winifred Carter
(17), of 25, Garnet Street, Cleethorpes,
she was riding her cycle with a friend
along Grimsby Road from Grimsby to
Cleethorpes, at 1-15 p.m., on 2nd January. When they were half-way across
Blundell Avenue a motor car, driven by
defendant from the opposite direction, began to turn in front of them into
Blundell Avenue without giving any
warning. Her friend avoided it, but
she was thrown from her cycle, which
was damaged. The car ran on the foot-
path near the Imperial Hotel.

Witnesses added that she was only
bruised and defendant took her home.

Cross-examined by Mr. Bloomer, she
agreed that she and her friend were
talking, but said they were looking
where they were going.

Corroborative evidence was given by
Irene Annie Crossland (16), of 22, Garnet
Street, who was cycling along with the
previous witness; Arthur Harris,
hawker, of 154, Grimsby Road; Charles
Henry Holmes, boilermaker, of 24, Duke
Street, Grimsby; Clifford Howard Cole-
brook, bricklayer's labourer, of 9,
Nicholson Street, Cleethorpes; and
Inspector Booth.

#### STATEMENT OF DEFENDANT.

The last named read a statement made
by defendant after the accident, in
which he said that his speed along
Grimsby Road was ten miles per hour,
and he slowed down to four miles when
he turned the corner into Blundell

---

## ROAD IMP

### Cyclists Like

A number of
schemes were consi
of the Cleetho
Wednesday night
perhaps, was the w
end of Grimsby F
was thought that a
of the cost would I
the Council had
view of the import
from the traffic p
Highways Commit
ported that infor
received from th
Engineer of the M
to the effect that
situated in a built-
possible to conside
upon a higher basi
The Committee
disappointment at
view of the urgent
recommended the C
County Council's
Cleethorpes Coun
fortieths of the inc
County Council the
On an estimate
£6,575 for the v
contributions woul
Transport £3,288,
Council £2,055 an
Council £1,232.
The Council agr
mendation, and the
the District Val
negotiation with th
required for the in

#### HEWITT'S

The Surveyor
temporary island
appeared to be f
torily, and it was
Highways Commit
copy of a resolutio
meeting of mem
Lincolnshire Bran
Touring Club urgi
to make the tempo
Hewitt's Circus a
and suggesting
roundabouts, where
points where road
facilitate speed."
Alderman W. F.
motorists had sugge
island would be m
circumference we
wondered if the
Highways Committe
the present size wa:
Alderman Sir G
that there were hu
about the matter.

---

'Police Officer Fined', *Grimsby News*, 1937. *Grimsby News*

brave enough to buy a bike to cycle to and from work. Bert knew all about the state of the driving tests at the time. He writes: 'The chap who joined with me had been a driving instructor in the army and he said he would teach me to drive if I did get a car.' The cost of obtaining a car was sky-high for Bert: £12.10s.0d and £5 to be paid three months later. That was for an Austin 7 Tourer. He received a ticking-off from his superiors for incurring a debt. Driving was a stress for anyone in that year of living dangerously.

The wider picture for car crime was, paradoxically, that there had been a fall in offences nationwide. In 1936, there had been 31,955 cases of careless driving and a 262 decrease in numbers of reckless driving. But the Home Secretary, Sir John Simon, acted in 1937 to improve things. Simon put 800 more mobile police officers on the roads, saying: 'For the experimental period it is proposed to quadruple the present motor patrol strength in areas selected . . .' Grimsby was not one of them, and it looks as though it should have been. The RAC saw that this enforcement was likely to help the effectiveness of the new Highway Code.

More seriously, was the issue of manslaughter. A Grimsby man, Mr Cross, escaped that fate, though he had killed a man while driving under the influence of drink. Just a few months after his offence, the House of Lords gave final authority to a ruling on what constituted manslaughter in deaths resulting from motor car accidents. The guideline was:

*In cases of manslaughter in driving motor cars . . . is a general rule of homicide by negligence. Simple lack of care, such as will consti- tute civil liability, is not enough. For purposes of the criminal law there are degrees of negligence and a very high degree of negligence is required to be proved before the felony is established.*

But Lord Atkin pointed out that 'a man may drive at a speed or in a manner dangerous to the public and cause death and yet not be guilty of manslaughter . . .'

That was why Mr Cross did not find himself away from his Grimsby home and in prison for ten years. But, of course, it can fairly confidently be asserted that the man suffered intensely from the thought that he had caused a death on the road. The 1937 'Year of Living Dangerously' in Grimsby was a curious mix of trivial collisions and horrible deaths.

# CHAPTER 26

# The Story of *The Girl Pat* Libel 1937–38

## The skipper was arrested and brought to England for trial

The story began simply enough. In May 1937 the fishing boat from Grimsby, *The Girl Pat*, arrived home in Portsmouth harbour after a long and adventurous journey around the world. The adventure had become so famous that the ship was to be put on display at Portsmouth in order to raise money for charity. But that was merely the quiet conclusion to the first part of the tale. After that, matters led to the High Court of Justice. Commander Lawrence said that she had taken him to the Azores and that despite being advised not to bring the ship home across the North Atlantic, he had made the trip in her, taking just eleven days. 'I have never been to sea in a better boat,' he commented.

But what was to follow led to a best-selling book and a high profile libel trial. Before that triumphant return, the ship had been stolen by her captain, Orsborne, and he and his crew set off on a long adventure in her. When Orsborne and his men were tracked down and arrested, they had what the newspapers at the time said was 'the effrontery to say that they were told to scuttle the ship and that rather than that, they ran away with her'. The skipper was arrested and brought back to England for trial.

The Central Criminal Court stepped in and demanded a police enquiry following that allegation. Orsborne was sent to prison, along with his brother. In order to back up their extra-ordinary allegation they said that the ship was damaged before they left and that she was not properly equipped for fishing, and that there was no food stored on board. Clearly, Orsborne's state-ment implied that a major fishing company, Marstrand's of Auckland Road Fish Docks in Grimsby, had done a damaging criminal action. Unfortunately for the *Daily Herald*, they had reported the statement, as had the publishers of a book about the case, Hutchinson and Co. Their book, *The Voyage of The Girl Pat* by Skipper Orsborne, had sold very well. The printers, The Anchor Press, were also involved. Marstrand had the famous Sir Patrick Hastings representing them, so they looked very likely to win damages, and indeed they did. Orsborne had said that he had been given instructions to scuttle the ship. That was a dramatic but untrue statement and the consequences were dire for the media involved.

At the heart of the concept of libel is that there has been 'the publication of false, defamatory words' and that the plaintiff must show that 'the statement made was defamatory and was made in the third person'. The skipper had said that his employers had told him to get rid of the trawler. Then there had been newspaper reports and a book. It was a story, true or not, too good to leave alone.

Hastings took delight in saying something about the 'Odd book' that had resulted from Orsborne's supposed adventures.

Hastings suggested that the book had been written by a journalist and that the captain was not capable of producing such writing anyway. The lawyer mentioned, for instance, that the ship had supposedly been to Devil's Island and that the captain had said he 'imagined it to be hell on earth'; but he had then added: 'It is far from that. It is a paradise. We live like gentlemen here.' There followed a peculiar account of the convict life there: 'Each convict has his own little bedroom . . . they rest during the noon day heat . . .'

If this had been written by the skipper when in gaol, then he had maybe been so imagina-

Sir Patrick Hastings. Author's collection

tive just to provide what he felt such a book should be about – in other words, that it must be a work of fiction. But there was no laughing matter when it came to the words provided by the publishers: 'Daredevil Dad Orsborne took the vessel out of Grimsby on an ostensible fishing trip only to decide when she had gained open sea to change her course and run her anywhere . . .'

Then the facts were given, rather than the fantasy. *The Times* reported:

> *The truth about* The Girl Pat *was that she was a trawler of about 25 tons, which was used for net fishing in shallow water. She was a new ship and had only just been overhauled when she was taken out by Orsborne. She had twelve days' supplies on board, there was a chart, the winch was in perfect order, and she was fully equipped.*

The rogue involved in those spurious memoirs had said that all those provisions were not available on board. When the managing director of Marstrand's was asked by Hastings what the effect on his company the allegations of the publishers would have, he replied: 'If I were a fisherman I would not enter employment with such a firm.' But the plaintiffs had gathered all necessary evidence, even to the extent of having a Danish seaman with a Master's certificate, who testified that the winch on the ship had been fine when he tested it. Things went from bad to worse for people involved in Marstrand's, including 'unpleasant social experiences'. Clearly, there had been bad feeling and also twisted and cruel humour around Grimsby when the story broke.

Another action was taken, this time against other papers. Journalists loved the idea that the ship might be undermanned and that there had been a directive to scuttle her. Some writers

# SKIPPER ORSBORNE
## The VOYAGE of the 'GIRL PAT'
Here is an adventure story the like of which has never before been heard in fact or fiction, and no one with a spark of romance left in them can afford to miss it With 17 illustrations (*Thursday*) 8/6

Advert for the offending book. *The Times*

made high drama of it all, and one writer even quoted some lines from Rudyard Kipling's poem, *The Ballad of the Bolivar* (1890) in which these lines appear:

> *Overloaded, undermanned, meant to founder, we Euchred God Almighty's storm, bluffed the eternal sea!*

There was no denying what that implied, amplifying the astounding accusations made by Orsborne.

The long fiasco ended with an abject apology from Valentine Holmes of the press charged with libel. He said that he desired on behalf of the defendants, publicly to express their deep regret for circulating the skipper's story. The Grimsby firm of solicitors, Deacon and Co, must have had some strange tales to tell when they went back north, as there had been almost as much drama in the High Court as there had been out at sea.

# Chapter 27

# Brawls and Incidents for the New Constable 1930s

## Three of us were involved in a punch-up with three miners from Doncaster . . .

Bert Fryer ended his police career as an Inspector. The newspaper article written to mark the end of his career noted that he had always lived by a personal motto: 'I shall pass through this world but once, therefore any good thing I can do to any human being, let me do it now. Let me not defer it or neglect it, for I shall not pass this way again.' Fryer came from a world of policing that is barely recognisable today. His career, though it involved plenty of unpleasantness, had a sprinkling of humour and entertainment in the streets and fields of Lincolnshire. He wanted to tell the press, when interviewed on his retirement, that he had always wanted to see the funny side of things.

Fryer started his police career in Cleethorpes. And he is one of the very few police officers who have written memoirs of the social history of the police work of their time. He started in Cleethorpes in 1937 – the year of all the motoring offences. His first bookings involved such minor events as a commercial traveller from Hull parking illegally and sorting out a few drunks. But then Fryer records some episodes in which we see a different side to life in Cleethorpes at a time when the laws of this land were very different. He reports a day when a body had been washed up on the foreshore. Fryer tries to express what it was like: 'I was told to go to the north end of the promenade . . . I had never before seen the dead body of a human being in my life, and started to scratch my head to try to remember what we had been told at Training School about dead bodies.'

Fryer found himself experiencing the events that follow on a suicide – still a crime in 1937. In the policeman's memoirs we

# LINCOLNSHIRE CONSTABULARY.

# INSTRUCTION BOOK.

Issued for the guidance of the
members of the above
Force.

Compiled

by

Chief Superintendent **W. TRIGG**, M.B.E.,

Deputy Chief Constable of Lincolnshire.

Hedley Slack & Co., Printers, 330, High Street, Lincoln.

Instruction Book for the Lincolnshire Constabulary. Author's collection

have the human side of things — the detail that he had to take sand out of the corpse's mouth 'to make him look presentable' whereas the *Grimsby Evening Telegraph* reported the business in a more objective way: 'How unemployment, following a bout of influenza, preyed on the mind of a Grimsby man and impelled him to take his own life was told to the Grimsby coroner today . . .'

In a contrasting situation, Fryer gives us an authentic account of what it must be like for a policeman to be involved in violent confrontation. He tells of a time when 'three of us were involved in a punch-up with three miners from Doncaster'. A gang of Doncaster men had made their day at the seaside a string of aggressive and disorderly events and attracted the notice of the law. On 30 July 1937, Fryer was on duty on the Kingsway at Cleethorpes when he received notice of a fight in Brighton Road. He found a crowd of people circled around two men covered in blood and fighting with considerable vigour.

Fryer, in plain clothes, stepped in, along with another colleague and Fryer managed to chain one of the offenders to the town hall railings. He notes that the crowd were hostile towards the police – then a strange thing happened. A woman pushed her

Police mobile column in the Grimsby area, 1960s. Lincolnshire Archives

way through the crowd and he asked her to go and ring for help, as Fryer and his other officers had no personal radios at that time.

The offenders were fined and given two days to find the money or go to prison. Fryer wrote that the men stayed with them until their relatives came from Doncaster. Fryer's attitude to all this was professional in the widest sense, meaning that he always reflected on the wider issues. Most of his work came from seasiders, let loose and going too far with their freedom to drink away from home. He writes that many of these drank heavily all day, mostly in the *Dolphin Hotel*, and so he spent plenty of time watching that place. But the level of recorded crime was not very

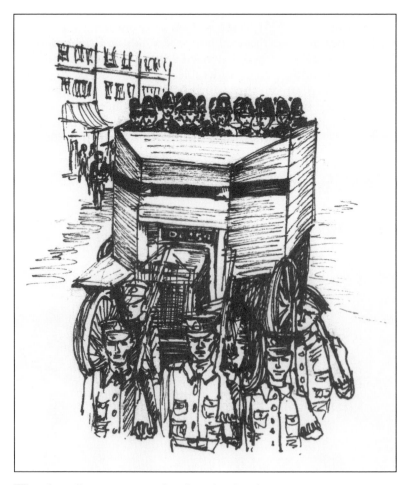

What the police were expected to do – riot situation. Laura Carter

high at the time. He notes, laconically, that at one time: 'Four weeks went by and I did not even catch cold.'

Even Fryer's training attached to the CID only led to a minor shoplifting incident. But overall Fryer's time at Cleethorpes, before he moved on to a country beat, opens up the life and crimes around a police constable in the 1930s – after all, a time of real hardship for many and of extremely violent crime in many parts of the land. His main thoughts on criminals were summed up in his reflection that: 'They get too much sympathy and publicity,' and he decried the hero-type media coverage many criminals had then. Fryer was policing at a time when the early talkies were just beginning to provide crime stories and the image of crooks was often glamorous. Even in a small place like Cleethorpes, though, he had his share of harsh experience.

● *Integrity, fairness and*

*social influence...*

# ...a police inspector

POLICE inspector B. E. Fryer, who retires tomorrow (Saturday), was praised at East Elloe Magistrates' Court, on Thursday for his integrity, fairness and social influence on the community.

Insp. Fryer says that through all the years he has served the public as a policeman, he has tried to live up to a motto he picked up in a sale room during the war.

It reads: "I shall pass through this world but once. Therefore any good thing I can do or any kindness I can show to any human being, let me do it now. Let me not defer it or neglect it, for I shall not pass this way again."

"I would say that is a good motto for any policeman," said Insp. Fryer.

### 'QUALITY'

Mr. E. R. Grief (chairman) said last Thursday that the Bench was aware of the high quality of the police force in this division "and Insp. Fryer is typical of the best."

Mr. Grief said Insp. Fryer was always scrupulously fair to the accused when he was prosecuting. On oehalf of the Bench, he thanked Insp. Fryer for his past services and wished him a 'ong and happy retirement.

Mr. G. A. Worth (deputy chairman) said Insp. Fryer had been a tremendous so 'ial influence in the district.

Mr. John Bowser (Clerk) said he felt sure that no accused person had left the court feeling he had been taken advantage of by Insp. Fryer. Nor had anyone left the court thinking they had "pulled the wool" over the prosecution's eyes.

Mr. George Hastings, on behalf of the advocates, praised Insp. Fryer's integrity as a policeman and his fairness as a prosecutor.

"It is a matter of sorrow for me that he is leaving."

### CHANGES

Talking to a "Guardian" reporter Insp. Fryer told of the changes in police work and the public's attitude.

In days gone by if louts were told to move on, and they did not, they were moved. Today, if this were the case, there would be a complaint

at the police station for assault.

The only person who suffered was the public, not the policeman. This, says Insp. Fryer, is where half the hooliganism starts.

He also decries the hero-type coverage given to criminals in the national Press: "They get too much sympathy and publicity." he said.

Perhaps the highlight of his career came with the famous Whaplode Drove exhumations in 1950.

Insp. Fryer is the longest serving officer in the Spalding division. Previously this distinction was held by the late Sgt. F. Brown, a close colleague of Insp. Fryer's.

### COMMENDED

Insp. Fryer has served under four superintendents in the division and has received commendations from the Chief Constable on six occasions.

Chief among his hobbies he numbers gardening and woodwork and has built two caravans in his spare time.

The start of his police career was at Cleethorpes on January 1, 1937. From there he moved to North Kelsey in March, 1939, then on to Holbeach Marsh in December of that year.

September, 1942, saw Constable Fryer in the Army. He started with the Coastal Artillery and ended up with the R.A.S.C. in Italy.

On November 25, 1945, he returned to Holbeach, where he served in the town area. moving to Swineshead in March, 1946, and to Spalding in March the following year, where he served as detective constable until February, 1950.

### PROMOTION

In that year he was made section sergeant at Holbeach and remained in that position until June, 1956 when he was promoted town inspector at Spalding, succeeding Insp. J. Sibbald.

Later, in June, 1960, when Insp. P. B. Wright retired, he took over the rural sub-division, the appointment he has held until his retirement.

Now he starts a new life as Diseases of Animals Inspector for Holland from January 1. He will make his home at "Strowan," Broadgate, Weston Hills.

● Insp. Fryer

## HE SEES THE FUNNY SIDE

INSP. Bert Fryer, whose retirement is reported elsewhere in this issue, has always been a man who can see the funny side of things.

He is a man, who, with a face as straight as a poker will tell an uproariously funny story.

Insp. Fryer is a man who has always had the respect of the editorial men of this office. They are sorry to see him go. His intimate knowledge of East Elloe will be missed.

## The "Finished Product" after 30 years service

# CHAPTER 28

# A Fuss Over a Thief's Appeal 1949

## Luckily for you, it is not a serious matter. I regard the crime as being more greed than anything else . . .

oseph Brook committed larceny in 1949, pleaded guilty, and was ordered to pay a total of £35. The Recorder stated that he would have to stay in custody until the fine was paid. Brook could not find the money, so he was placed in custody for twenty-five days. That should have been straightforward, but a new Act had been introduced in 1948. This allowed lawyers for Brook to argue that the recorder should never have imposed the confinement.

Brook wanted his pound of flesh. He had been locked up for a considerable time for what he thought of as a trivial offence. The Criminal Justice Act of 1948 made it mandatory for a court to allow time for a sum to be paid but also laid down a ruling that the custodial sentence had to be a fixed period of not more than a year. The Recorder at Grimsby did not give a fixed term for the imprisonment.

There was Brook, in HMP Lincoln, wondering if he would ever see the light of day again. But, as there was a case for the Grimsby error, his story ended up being told and examined before two of the most famous judges in Britain: Sir Norman Birkitt and Travers Humphries.

Brook was a ship's cook and he had stolen goods from the ship's stores. He had come ashore with a pound of pork, quite large amounts of bacon, flour, fruit and some currants. The total value of the lot was around eleven shillings – hardly a matter for learned men of the silk. But his character was not without blemish since he had previous convictions. At Grimsby Quarter Sessions, the Recorder had maintained that he would not send Brook to prison, saying: 'Luckily for you it is not a serious matter.

I regard the crime as being more greed than anything else.' But he then went on to impose a fine and costs, totalling £35. Then came the fatal words: 'You will remain in custody until it is paid.' The defence lawyer had said, rather too confidently: 'My client can raise, I think, £10 . . . tomorrow if not today . . .' He upset the Recorder who was having no exceptions and would not listen to what was going to be an appeal for payments to be made later. He said: 'I am not entering into any instalment plan.'

The lawyer tried another ploy, saying: 'The difficulty is, he lives in Leeds.'

'Then the difficulty must be overcome,' said the Recorder, 'I am not letting him free from this court.'

That was the end of it. The Recorder must have been having a bad day. Off went Brook from the court, languishing in gaol for the twenty-five days and then he wrote to the Recorder, pointing out that he still did not have the money. The Recorder released him until he could appear at the next quarter sessions. Brook made vigorous efforts to raise cash. Before the new Act, a man in Brook's position would have gone to gaol and then petitioned the Crown. Many men in that situation would then have been released, the days inside being considered punishment enough for such a minor offence.

Brook had stirred up a nest of vipers. The lawyers acting for him saw the error of the Recorder and set to work on an appeal. It entailed looking at a law going right back to 1822 and another of 1859, both detailing that a man in Brook's position would be considered a debtor to the Crown and time would be given to raise money. At the appeal, Humphreys said: 'How he (the Recorder) could assume that a man in his position remaining in custody could find £25 I do not know, but that is what he did.'

It was all a learning experience for professionals involved in courts of quarter sessions; they would have to say that they could fine a person a certain figure and set three instalments, or set a prison sentence with a term. The noble Lords set Brook free with the comment: 'We think in this case the appellant has been sufficiently punished for what he did. We therefore quash the sentence . . . and he goes free from today.'

Brook must have surely left the court with a smile on his face. His petty theft had caused quite a stir.

# Chapter 29

# Robbery With Violence
# 1953

## The old woman was bound, gagged and robbed in her own home . . .

In Grimsby Magistrates' Court an old woman of eighty-seven years told those present that she had endured the horrendous experience of having an assailant spring out at her from a corner of her own home. Mrs Mary Humphrey of Weelsby Road said that she had been struck with a pair of heavy brass fire-tongs. Most unusually, her attacker was a young woman of twenty-three.

'She tried to put a scarf around my neck and I thought she was going to strangle me,' Mrs Humphrey said. She was robbed of £208 but that loss was surely nothing compared to the mental anguish of the assault. Her attacker was Bridget O'Callaghan, who had broken into the old woman's home and hidden herself, ready to pounce when the time was right. Those familiar words – 'she was of no fixed address' – were used to describe the vicious criminal. Mrs Humphrey was a widow, aged and very vulnerable. The method of attack was extremely callous. Mr Ward, prosecuting, said that Mrs Humphrey was the type who should 'command respect' in any but 'the most callous and cruel person.'

The attack was at Christmas time, on 21 December. When the victim was taken to hospital, Dr Patrick Pearson tended her, and in court he said: 'When I saw her she was suffering from three small lacerations on the back of the head; one of these was stitched, and one on her forehead, which was stitched. She had wounds on her fingers and wrist as well; her left eye was black.' These were all signs of a brutal and relentless physical attack. Although the injuries were classified as of 'moderate severity' it was realised by everyone involved that the real scars were mental ones. From that day on, her own home would be a place of fear.

Weelsby Road. Lincolnshire Archives

The victim told the court that in the weeks since the attack her hearing had deteriorated. On the night in question she bolted the drawing room door – a room in which there was a French window (always more vulnerable to burglary). It then emerged in court that, as was so often the case with older people, Mrs Humphrey kept a considerable sum of money at home. She had well over £60 kept in a jug, all in bank notes. All seemed well, but it was next morning when she received the awful shock of an attack. She unbolted the doors and at around half past ten she opened the drawing room door and stepped inside, then as she said: 'I could not have got very far because as soon as I stepped inside I saw the brass fire-tongs coming down on my head.'

After Mrs Humphrey was hit, she managed to see the figure of O'Callaghan standing over her and said: 'Why have you done this to me?' It says a lot for the despicable nature of the attacker that she stood in court looking very different, having made every effort to appear different, knowing that the old woman's eyesight was bad. Mrs Humphrey, being asked if she could see her attacker in the court, said that she thought it was O'Callaghan but that 'she looks very different . . . She looked stouter and she had no lipstick on.'

The young thug then asked for money and the poor old woman said that she had none whereupon O'Callaghan had made her head bleed. Poor Mrs Humphrey at the time was clearly finding it hard to account for the fact that a young woman had done such a brutal thing, as she asked if the young brute had thought that it was a man opening the door. O'Callaghan assented to that and then asked for some hot water so that she

Feature from the local paper on the attack on Mrs Humphrey. *Scunthorpe Evening Telegraph*

could bathe her victim's head. As O'Callaghan went back into the other room to get her bag, Mrs Humphrey had the presence of mind to pick up some small change and offer it to O'Callaghan, who had already filled a large bag with anything that seemed worth stealing. The latter repeated her demands for money and said: 'If you scream I will murder you.' She then tried torture, extorting information from her aged victim, screwing her arm around and hitting her in the face with her fist.

At that point Mrs Humphrey must have virtually passed out. She told the court that after the pummelling she had lost feeling in part of her face and her eyes were painful. Things went from bad to worse, as the attacker became more and more desperate to get details of any hidden cash. She put a scarf around the old woman's neck and then took violent hold of her throat with her hand. It was then that Mrs Humphrey was tied and gagged; her hands were tied with the scarf and an apron used to tie the feet. Then poor Mrs Humphrey passed out. When she was faintly aware that she could hear movement, she kept quiet, for fear of being hit again, and she recalled hearing O'Callaghan saying she had been upstairs and found nothing there.

Later, Mrs Humphrey managed to move slowly into her kitchen and then, as she summoned some strength, managed to find some scissors with which she snipped the scarf and freed herself. 'I lay a long time in front of the fire,' she told the court. Some time afterwards, as she had the power to move about, and she had realised that her tormentor had left her, she threw some coal at her neighbour's door, and he came to help her. Mrs Humphrey had fought for her life and had been through prolonged torture.

As for Bridget O'Callaghan, she was committed for trial at Lincoln Assizes and a long prison sentence waited for her, although there was a demand that she be examined by a psychologist. It was a time when attacks on vulnerable old people were very common. In the early to mid-1950s over twenty cases of elderly women living alone being ruthlessly attacked were recorded in the country. Many of them were shopkeepers who were attending their premises alone. But in this Grimsby case, the unusual feature was the attack from within the woman's own home – a place that should have been the safest place on earth for her.

This was one of the most callous crimes in the records of Grimsby crime. It was entirely typical of this 'new order' of violence. Something caused a dramatic change in the nature of violent crime against the person in the 1950s. Arguably, it was the time when psychopaths and sociopaths became labelled and discussed. The fact that assailants could be within the private, domestic sphere was terrifying. Stories abounded in the popular press that people should have for 'healthy self-protection'. It was an age of paranoia in one sense, but in another, it was justified to make people aware of those changes. Only a few years before the Humphrey attack a man had kidnapped a young woman and imprisoned her under her floorboards, forcing her to dig out her own den from the soil. She was only found after writing 'Help' on a stick and ramming it through flower beds.

O'Callaghan brought that kind of fear to Grimsby. Her victim was frail and helpless and the regime of terror inflicted by her was intense, heartless and merciless. At that time the response was to explore the notion of 'diminished responsibility', a concept causing long and heated debate in the rooms of lawyers and in

Lincoln Crown Court. The author

the courts. A crime like O'Callaghan's was so extreme that the immediate search for a reason was in the realms of abnormal psychology. A person had to be 'ill' to inflict such pain and torment, yet the newspapers were happier to use words such as 'evil' and 'demented'.

# CHAPTER 30

# Indecency at the Seaside?
# 1954

## Police raids resulted in the arrest and prosecution of both publishers and artists

Donald McGill was the artist who produced the famous saucy postcards once found at all English seaside resorts. The humour of his cards was one of the treats of being on holiday and thousands were sent home by people who were relishing their time in the sun or in the pub. A typical card was one showing a scene in a bedroom in which a busty and scantily-clad blonde says to her lover: 'Blimey, here's my husband – can you come back tonight?' The man, looking suitably flushed and disturbed, is the stereotypical milkman, and replies: 'What in my own ruddy time – are you kidding missus!'

But, in the 1950s, McGill and his publishers were in trouble. The images and jokes were running into problems with the obscene publications legislation. He had experienced trouble before then, but not very often. McGill once said, with this trouble in mind: 'During the whole period of my career the authorities have made no complaints about the postcards drawn by me, with the following exceptions: in or about 1906 I recollect that an order was made for the destruction of a very large number of cards in the North of England; in or about 1920 proceedings were taken against the retailers of cards but no order was made . . .'

It comes as a shock to read about the problems in 1954, because McGill had the status of being recognised and complimented by no less a literary figure than George Orwell, whose essay, *The Art of Donald McGill* appeared 1941. In a letter to Anthony Powell in 1947, Orwell was well aware of the likelihood of offence caused by the cards when he said: 'Thanks so much for your postcard which I think was rather lucky to get here – at any rate I think the crofter who brings the post the last seven miles might have suppressed it if he had seen it.' Orwell was living on the Isle of Jura, and he feared that the community there were too austere and morally righteous to accept the kind of ribald humour on a McGill card.

After the return to government of the Conservatives in 1951 there was a moral reaction to the slippage in 'standards of morality' in the arts as it was perceived at the time. In the five years following that date 167,000 books were censored. It was only a matter of time before attention turned to the saucy postcard. At the time there were 'watch committees' at seaside resorts, and Cleethorpes was no exception. It was a regular occurrence to have complaints voiced against postcards, as many people considered them to be lewd rather than harmless fun. It was inevitable that there would be police raids on premises where cards might be in stock, and actions began to be taken in Grimsby. Police raids resulted in the arrest and prosecution of both publishers and artists.

The Grimsby County Petty Sessional Division court issued writs on behalf of the Director of Public Prosecutions against manufacturers who produced the McGill cards. The wording of the summons related to 'unlawfully publishing an obscene postcard named Donald McGill Comics no. 811'. The Cleethorpes Chamber of Trade was worried too. In 1953 the Honorary Secretary wrote to Messrs D Constance Ltd in London in order to find out about the circulation and distribution of the cards because, 'seventeen shops in the town were raided by the police'. The Secretary added that: 'Quantities of comic cards were taken away, so no doubt proceedings will follow to the annoyance to every one of the traders concerned.' Information was also required as to whether cards in Cleethorpes were typical of the merchandise distributed elsewhere. Obviously, if there were a set range of cards going to every town, then there would be a massive number of raids and potential prosecutions.

This legal action stemmed from the 1857 Obscene Publications Act. The local outcome was a prominent trial in Lincoln on 15 July 1954. McGill's own defence was that in most of the images he had 'no intention of double meaning and in fact in some cases, a double meaning was pointed out to me . . .' However, he was found guilty and had to pay £50 in a fine and £25 in costs. Large numbers of cards were then destroyed and many of the smaller postcard producers were ruined.

The onslaught against publishers and shopkeepers was relentless. In Brighton, in July 1953, magistrates ordered the destruction of 113 out of 175 varieties of postcards. One of the defendants spoke up on behalf of the general grievances felt by seaside traders when he said: 'You are a kind of Arts Council on this matter. When the Obscene Publications Act of 1857 was passed, England was worrying about Napoleon (he needed a history lesson) and standards of morality were lower than today.' One merchant conceded that the cards were sometimes 'a little near the knuckle' but the most that could be said in criticism was that there was innuendo in both the image and the text.

At that time, people in Cleethorpes had been more worried by recent floods and extremely bad weather, but the affair certainly disturbed the normal equanimity of the Cleethorpes traders. As for George Orwell, he had his own defence of McGill: 'The comic postcards are one expression of his point of view, a humble one, less important than the music halls, but still worthy of attention. In a society which is still basically Christian they naturally concentrate on sex jokes . . . Their whole meaning and virtue is their unredeemed lowness. They stand for the worm's eye view of life . . .'

In other words, as with all humour of the baser kind, they remind us of the absurdity of moral strictness to the extent of denying communication about such topics as sex. But that view was too advanced for the austere world of 1950s' Britain. With hindsight, it would be easy to see this case as a storm in a tea cup – something rather more eccentric than important. But in fact the reasoning behind the bans was the significant factor. Here was a case in which a harmless and titivating ingredient of the English seaside experience was removed for the sake of 'decency'. Today, modern political correctness has no room for what was then merely considered by most people to be 'saucy' in a way like the *Carry On* films.

But the McGill case turned out to be little more than yet another instance of what Lord Macaulay called, sarcastically, a 'fit of morality': 'We know of no spectacle so ridiculous as the British public in one of its periodical fits of morality.' Naturally, at the time, it brought out yet again the debate about what is art and what is smut. Only six years after this fiasco Britain would

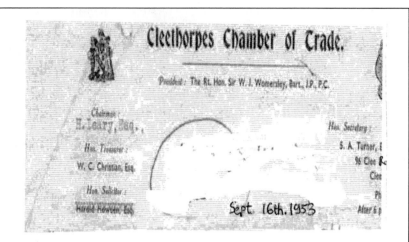

Cleethorpes Chamber of Trade.

President : The Rt. Hon. Sir W. J. Womersley, Bart., J.P., P.C.

Chairman :
H. Leary, Esq.,

Hon. Treasurer :
W. C. Christian, Esq.

Hon. Solicitor :
Harold Newton, Esq.

Hon. Secretary :
S. A. Turner,

Sept. 16th. 1953

Messrs. D. Constance Ltd.,
22, Christ Church Rd.,
LONDON, S.W.8.

Re: Donald McGill Comic Cards

Dear Sirs,

On Friday of last week seventeen shops in this town were
Raided by police and quantities of comic cards were taken away. No doubt
Proceedings will follow to the annoyance of everyone who is concerned.

One of our members has given your name as one of the
Largest firms dealing in this class of business, and after discussing this matter
With the committee, I have been asked to write to you for your co-operation
In an endeavour to put this matter on a fair basis.

My Chamber would like to know if the class of comic cards
supplied to Mr Hallett and to other traders in the town is similar to those supplied
in other towns; and we understand that no action of a similar kind has been taken

Your early reply is awaited with interest

Thanking you
Yours faithfully,

Letter from the Cleethorpes Chamber of Trade. Courtesy of the Chamber archivist

have to cope with the attempt to understand the *Lady Chatterley's Lover* trial. Like the McGill case, it would seem to many to be little more than victimisation on the part of the 'jobsworth' attitude. Nevertheless, it is difficult today to bring to mind the kind of apprehensions felt by ordinary people, running their small business, in such a strange moral climate.

# CHAPTER 31

# Seaman on a Crime Spree
# 1954

**I took the tug *Fearnought* from Rochester. I intended taking it to the continent but the bearings got hot . . .**

Williiam Fowler, aged thirty-one, from Barry in South Wales, stood in the dock at Grimsby charged with having a revolver in his possession when arrested. He had also stolen a tug as part of his crime spree. The bench decided that there was a strong possibility of insanity here and recommended an examination to discover the relevant facts. But Fowler was still committed for trial in Lincoln.

The spree had been full of incident, but Fowler's arrest was something of an anti-climax, as he had merely been found breaking and entering a shop and garage in Grimsby. When taken, by Detective Sergeant Bateman, Fowler admitted a string of other offences, including stealing a bicycle at Byfleet in Surrey and several thefts in Norfolk. In Grimsby, he had simply taken a key and ten shillings; but the day after his arrest he talked about stealing the tug, and he also explained where he obtained his gun. It had been stolen from a bungalow at Horning, or somewhere with a name like that, he claimed. It was all an odd mixture of vagueness and nastiness. His account was garbled and fantastic. Fowler said: 'I took the tug *Fearnought* from Rochester. I intended taking it to the continent but the bearings got hot . . .'

However, Detective Sergeant Bateman had had a hard time bringing the man in. He told the Grimsby magistrates that he had fought with Fowler, knowing the man had a gun. Fowler had broken into a garage at Algernon Street in Grimsby, and taken the key and money from a Mr Bradley. Fowler was a heavily-built man, and he was wearing a blue suit when DS Bateman saw him on the docks in the early evening. The police officer had been making enquiries all day and now he had his man in sight. Fowler was just about to get on a Hull train when he was approached by DS Bateman. The latter knew of Fowler's physical description at the time, but not his name. When the detective went up to him he asked his name, Fowler replying: 'Johansson, and I'm from Cardiff.'

The first interchange of words was awkward to say the least. Bateman then said: 'I'm putting you under arrest.' 'You're not – I have a job to go to in Hull,' Fowler replied.

DS Bateman knew he had to act fast, and there was a suspicion that the man might be armed, so he grabbed him and tried to put him in restraint. Fowler was very strong and, luckily for the detective, three railwaymen came to his assistance. The gun was in Fowler's hip pocket, and DS Bateman explained that, even with the other men helping, the weapon could not be taken, and they forced him towards the porter's room.

It was when help arrived, in the form of PC Lyons, that the group finally restrained and controlled Fowler and the gun was taken from him. Bateman showed the court the .22 calibre American revolver he took from the villain on the run. 'There were six cartridges in the chambers, and a further sixty-two cartridges of the same calibre on him,' DS Bateman said. When charged, at first Fowler said nothing but later went into his long account of the theft of the tug and all the other crimes done down the East coast.

When detained and seen by Inspector Purser, Fowler said that he wanted to be sent to prison. Purser gave the obvious answer that there were hundreds of questions to put to this enigmatic character and so going to see him repeatedly in Lincoln prison was out of the question. It was with great attention to detail that Purser reported to the court just how much Fowler would be looked after. It seems that there was a general awareness that the man was not 'all there' mentally. Fowler was making a fuss about being kept warm as he thought that he would be warm in prison rather than in a police cell. The magistrate took up this point, to be told by Purser that everything would be done to keep the man comfortable.

Fowler definitely needed care, for himself as well as for others. In his crazy narrative of what he had done while drifting across country, stealing where he could – he even talked about running the stolen tug aground on the Isle of Sheppey. If Fowler's long and complex tale was true, and that he really had wandered across the counties from Essex to Humber doing mischief, then it was just plain bad luck that the man had concluded his spree

Headline on the case. *The Times*

## SEAMAN FOR TRIAL ON REVOLVER CHARGE

### ALLEGED CONFESSION TO TAKING TUG

William J. H. Fowler, aged 31, seaman, of Romilly Road, Barry Docks, South Wales, at Grimsby yesterday, was committed for trial at Lincoln Assizes, charged with having a revolver in his possession at the time of his arrest on September 29, breaking and entering a Grimsby store and stealing 10s. and a key, and breaking and entering a garage, with intent to steal. Detective-sergeant A. Bateman said in evidence that at the police station Fowler admitted the offences at Grimsby and in an alleged statement he admitted that he stole a bicycle at Byfleet, Surrey, and committed several thefts in the Suffolk area.

The following day he made another alleged statement in which he said that he got the revolver and ammunition from a bungalow at Horning, Horningsea, or Horsey. He also said: " I took the tug Fearnought from Rochester. I intended to take it to the Continent, but the bearings got hot King's Lynn way and I beached her on the Isle of Sheppey."

Mr. P. Gladwin, who appeared for Fowler, asked that before Fowler took his trial he should be examined mentally.

The magistrates agreed to that.

by being a problem for Grimsby. Many then were of the opinion that Fowler would have made a first-class storyteller – except for his penchant for guns.

Again, it was a crime of its time. That period was brimming over with stories about crime sprees; something about the impact of B movies and adventure stories explains the typical tale of a man on the rampage. Films like *The Thirty-Nine Steps* made the notion of being 'on the road' and free appealing. The main exception in this case was that the man who ended up in Grimsby with a gun really was armed and dangerous – unpredictable and whimsical, ready for any danger and risk. The town was indeed fortunate that in its police force it had men capable of handling that explosive situation. Of course, the feature of the arrest is that there were public employees ready to 'have a go' and help the police. Again, that was a feature of the time. Even in some of the major crime stories then, such as the 'Battle of Heathrow' in 1948 when Scotland Yard took on the London gangs in an attempted airport heist, members of the public joined in – but so very different from today.

# CHAPTER 32

# Bravery at Gunpoint
# 1955

## He advanced on the armed Grimsby youth . . .

There are famous heroes and there are ordinary heroes. Most communities remember the former but the latter are usually forgotten. Hopefully this chapter will help Grimsby recall a quiet hero, a man from an event over fifty years ago. He was called Henry Frow and he kept a garage in Barnetby.

What Henry Frow did was risk his life in confronting a gunman. He advanced on an armed Grimsby youth and played his part in the resolution of the drama. Brian Smith, of Earl Street in Grimsby, was just eighteen at the time, and had no alternative in court but to plead guilty to attempted murder. He had pointed his gun at Frow, of Hilltop Garage, who intervened in an abduction. It all began early on an August morning, when Smith got into a taxi driven by a Mr Thickett and told him to take him to Bradley crossroads. It became a horrific experience for the driver, as Smith rapped out the command that he should drive on, shouting: 'Now you're taking me to Leeds!' It was like a scene from a gangster B movie, and was followed by a warning: 'Don't make any false moves if you value your life.'

The prosecution, led by Mr Corley, made a point of stressing just how intense was Smith's insistent string of threats, making Mr Thickett terrified for his life. The gunman said: 'You have a wife and kids at home and you want to get back to them, I'm sure.' Then it was urgent that they stop for some petrol, near Barnetby.

As Frow's wife came out to attend to them, Smith rapped out an order for the driver to stay inside the vehicle and to pay from his seat. As Mrs Frow then went around the back of the car, just for a few seconds the gunman's glare was off the man in front and he bolted for cover well away from his taxi. Naturally, Mrs Frow shouted for help at that point, as something was clearly

# 'Great courage' of garageman

## 'ADVANCED ON ARMED GRIMSBY YOUTH'

FACED by a youth armed with a sawed-off shotgun, a North Lincolnshire garage proprietor behaved with "extreme courage," it was stated at Lincolnshire Assizes today.

Brian Edward Smith (18), of 12, Earl-street, Grimsby, pleaded not guilty to attempting to murder the garage proprietor, Mr. Henry Arthur Frow, of Hilltop Garage, Barnetby, on August 27.

He pleaded guilty to two other charges—having a firearm in his possession with intent to endanger life, and attempting to use it in resisting arrest.

Mr. M. E. F. Corley, prosecuting, said that the story began at Grimsby at 6.30 p.m. on August 27 when Smith hailed a taxi, got in, and told the driver, a Mr. Thickett, to drive to Bradley Cross-roads.

He drove there and then said to the driver: "Now you are taking me to Leeds. Put your foot down and get cracking. Don't make any false moves if you value your life."

### 'Various threats'

Mr. Corley declared: "Under this threat Mr. Thickett drove in the direction of Leeds. On the way Smith made various threats such as 'You have a wife and kids at home, you would like to get back to them I am sure.' The petrol was getting low and the taxi driver had

**MR. FROW**
". . . extreme courage."

to stop at Mr. Frow's garage. Mr. Corley said Mrs. Frow came out, and Smith ordered Mr. Thickett not to leave the car, and to pay for the petrol from his seat. As Mrs. Frow went to the back of the car something distracted Smith's attention, and the driver jumped out and ran for cover.

Mr. Frow heard his wife shout, and came downstairs. He reached the door and saw Smith running after the taxi driver.

Mr. Frow's behaviour was extremely creditable. He not only stood his ground, but he advanced towards Smith.

### 'Took a blow'

Mr. Frow continued advancing towards the prisoner, who pointed the gun at him. Mr. Frow took a blow on his wrist from the gun. He knocked the gun up, and thereby saved his life. It might be that Smith did not intend to fire, but it remains that the gun went off.

"Having fired this one round Smith then went into the forecourt to look for other transport," continued Mr. Corley.

"It happened that another car driven by a Mr. Blackbourne and carrying his wife and daughter drove up.

"Smith ordered the two women to get out and forced Mr. Blackbourn to drive on with him along the road. It appears that Smith managed to reload his gun, because a fired cartridge was found in the car.

Smith was in the front seat and he held the gun on Mr. Blackbourn, who in turn, had to get some more petrol and drove to a filling station at Wrawby.

### 'Not fast'

"Mr. Blackbourn was unable to get away, as the driver had done. They drove on again, and it appears that Mr. Blackbourn prevailed on Smith to get out, explaining that it was a small car and not fast for getting away.

The prisoner got out.

"Meanwhile Mr. Frow had not lost his presence of mind. He jumped into his own sports car, and followed, going to Brigg police station.

He said the police began a search for Smith, who was overtaken on the road by P.c.s Wright and Green. He ran into a field.

### 'No notice'

"These two officers behaved with considerable courage. On being chased the accused turned and threatened them with the gun but they took no notice, and, as they were on him, he threw down the gun.

"They found it was loaded and the accused had seven other cartridges in his possession." said Mr. Corley.
(Proceeding)

## After whales

The second of the three Japanese whaling fleets, which make up Japan's

**Join the many at the Midland**

wrong with the two men in the car, and Mr Frow came outside.

Frow saw immediately that Smith was chasing the driver, and that he had a gun. He bravely walked towards Smith, cool and assured. Smith cracked him on the wrist with the gun, and then Frow was close enough to act. He knocked the gun upwards and it fired. There is no telling what would have happened had he not acted at that moment. The result was that Smith, as his round was fired then, moved off swiftly to find some other vehicle to commandeer. The reign of terror was not over and the young man had another round to reload his gun.

This time the unlucky driver to meet Smith in this mood was Mr Blackbourn, and he was with his wife and daughter in their car. The women were ordered out of the car and Smith set off, pointing the gun at Blackbourn. This time, he was sitting in the front seat. Again, they had to stop for petrol, this time at Wrawby. Blackbourn was a good talker and used his wits. He made it clear that his little car was not exactly the kind of vehicle a man would choose to effect a getaway, and that must have appealed to Smith's sense of drama. He was a man who had watched too many movies. Smith stepped from the car and then anything could have happened – except that Henry Frow was not finished with his would-be attacker.

Frow had alerted the law and police officers were now in pursuit. Soon, Smith was cornered, running into a field, with officers Wright and Green after him. Again, here was a situation in which a young thug threatened men with his gun, and again, threats did not meet with a response of fear. Smith was finally overpowered. He was destined for a long prison sentence.

Henry Frow deservedly made the headlines. Maybe many would have said he acted foolishly, putting his life on the line, but without his act of courage, who can tell what might have happened, and what Smith might have done with the gun.

Guns were still around at that time, survivals from the war. Thousands of revolvers had been brought home and, in spite of periodic amnesties, weapons were still around and easy to find and use. When organised gangs used them, there might be some kind of code of practice, but nothing legislated for the individual dreamer, psychopath or deranged kid. In whichever category we try to place Smith, nothing takes away from the bravery of Frow, a man who not only protected his own, by sheer instinct, but also took an active part in the chase for the fugitive.

Barnetby, a small place where not much happens, was not exactly a village with a peaceful image at the time. Not long after this, a young woman pulled up on a bike and walked into a post office, threatening to shoot someone. In the decade or so after the end of the war, the post office's position 'on the road' where people might stop for petrol or refreshments, might have been good for local trade, but the other side of that was a dark one – it was a place where men like Smith would be tempted to stop (or forced to stop) and mayhem might follow. On this occasion, the right man for the job was on the spot, cool, calm and brave. A quiet, dependable local man had done things 'beyond the call of duty' that day, which started with the routine of every other day, and ended like a car-chase scene from Hollywood.

# CHAPTER 33

# A Vagrancy Issue
# 1955

## ... the mere sight of the document would show that the appellant was a man with a long list of convictions ...

The problem of homeless drifters has been a nagging problem for English law since the first poor laws and vagrancy statutes of the Elizabethan period but, by the 1950s, tramps, drifters and generally suspicious looking types were a thorn in the flesh in a different way. A case in Grimsby highlighted the difficulties of dealing with vagrants.

In English criminal law, a person standing charged with an offence has to be tried on the grounds of that specific offence, and nothing else beyond that. Courts in the past have often run into trouble and made mistakes because of contravening that rule. In the case of a known criminal in Grimsby a mistake was made.

In October 1955, Mr Fitzwalter Buller found himself acting for a group of people whose property had been under threat from a 'vagrant' named Fuller. It was going to be a simple matter to show that the man had been up to no good on some premises, as the Recorder at the quarter sessions in Grimsby had been given a long list of the man's previous convictions. That was a step that the aggrieved parties may have regretted because the case went to the Court of Appeal.

It was a case of a record of a known 'bad character' being given in court to prejudice a decision. Fuller had been asked why he had not accepted work, as he had not appeared in court at an earlier time. Then, on the night in question, he had been found in a place where he was almost certainly going to commit an offence.

The drifter was a man who had caused a series of confrontations with the local police and he was often under observation. It was known that he was the type who could easily shift from minor offences to other, more serious ones, and when he was caught and charged on this particular occasion, that thinking lay behind the police actions. But it was in the court that things went wrong for everyone concerned, and all because of a too enthusiastic court official.

"'OW ARE YER? PRETTY BOBBISH, EH?"

The 'Sus laws' long ago. *Punch*

Fuller had been given a three-month prison sentence, under the old Vagrancy Act of 1824, so there was a feeling of certainty that he was out to do a burglary or even worse. But, as the Appeal Court noted, to haul him up in court and then place the list of convictions in front of the judge was malpractice. The judge at appeal said: 'The merest glance at the report by anyone accustomed to that class of document, would show that he was dealing with what might be called "an old hand".' The mere sight of the document, it was said, would show that the appellant was a man with a long list of previous convictions.

The outcome was that if there was an appeal, then no details of previous convictions should be made visible. The man had gone to prison on what in legal terms is called an 'unsafe' judgement. Clearly, this all became a matter of prejudice, and that was not difficult to show before the High Court Judge, Mr Justice Ormerod.

Here was a case of a 'bad character' who, nevertheless, found himself languishing in gaol because he had received a 'punishment' for things allegedly done well before his latest appearance in court. Maybe his defence in court – that he had been on the property when he was arrested looking for work – did not really convince the magistrate, but he was badly handled, and that was the bottom line.

The fateful list, given to the Recorder, could not have been put in front of a jury, and so a basic principle of law had been breached. The basis of the debate was in the operation of the so-called 'Sus laws' and these were common causes of discontent at the time. The famous detective Jack Slipper, on the streets at the same time as the Grimsby event, has this to say about these laws which enabled officers to stop anyone 'on suspicion': 'As I became more experienced I had a number of good arrests, thanks to the Section Four of the 1824 Vagrancy Act which allows a police officer to arrest someone he suspects of being about to commit an arrestable offence. That doesn't mean you can pick up someone just because you might be a criminal . . .'

In other words, the Grimsby affair happened largely because the officers concerned knew the man in question.

# Double Murder
# 1959

## There had been a series of attacks across north-east Lincolnshire

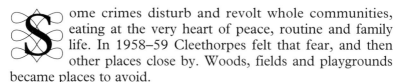

Some crimes disturb and revolt whole communities, eating at the very heart of peace, routine and family life. In 1958–59 Cleethorpes felt that fear, and then other places close by. Woods, fields and playgrounds became places to avoid.

Just before Christmas in 1958 police were concerned about a spate of attacks on children around the Grimsby area. The net of investigation was cast wide, as there had been a series of attacks across north-east Lincolnshire. Early the next year, in February, Linda Brown, just six, went to play with her older brother in Weelsby Woods, a public park between Grimsby and Cleethorpes. They were playing the usual innocent games when a young man came along and joined in. After a while, little Linda walked away with the youth, ostensibly to gather sticks. Young David became worried when Linda did not come back and soon a police search was in progress.

At half past six the worst outcome, feared by everyone, became a horrible fact. Linda had been killed, and she had also been raped. Superintendent Tew wanted to make sure that part of his announcement for local people was a statement that this crime was linked to other attempted attacks or smaller scale ones in the area. There was a description of the stranger, of course. David and others had spent some time with him as he played with everyone. He was in his late teens, with dark hair and there was a strong feeling that he was out of work. The campaign began around the town, because police were sure that the killer was a local man. 'Where was your son on Monday?' was a question asked a thousand times in a few days.

There was a sighting. A local man said he had seen a person

like the one described by the police loitering in the area where the killing took place, so more descriptive details were gathered. There were fine details – down to the tie he wore having three small sequins, black greasy hair and a pointed nose. By 2 March an arrest was made – an unemployed man named Herbert Scott, staying in Mangle Street, Grimsby. He had no fixed address, and to some extent he fitted the description. Scott was stood before the judge at Lincoln Assizes on 2 June. Victor Durand, prosecuting, noted that one fact was important – that the boy who came home to raise the alarm noticed that the time was 3.20. This was important because an adult had seen Scott play with the children just twenty minutes beforehand.

Durand recounted the events, from the brother and sister meeting the man, who was smoking and asked for a light, to the point at which the man and Linda went away to gather firewood. There were a few observed details, such as the fact that the man had been reading 'a white book' at one point. The young brother did find the man and he asked him if he had seen Linda. He replied: 'No, I thought she was on the swing with you.'

Little Linda had been struck by a milk bottle and there was a large bruise on her head, then she had died from asphyxia after inhaling vomit. The sexual attack was the outrage that incensed the community.

Checking Scott's movements and whereabouts that day, police found that he had been in Grimsby from 4.30 to 5.45. He insisted that he had not been to Weelsby Woods, but a 'white book' was found in his possession, though that is only circumstantial. More convincing was the fact that the police had wisely arranged for an alternative to the traditional identity parade. They had asked David and another boy present on the day of the murder to observe movements of people in Mangle Street and both pointed to Scott. Eventually Scott made a confession, recounting his talk with his father in Riby Square at the Seaman's Mission and then going to the woods, 'to see if they changed since I was a boy'. Scott described meeting the children and then talking to Linda, admitting that he asked her to pull down her underclothes; and said that he 'accidentally killed her' and lost his senses.

For the defence, Ling Mallison pointed out that there was another suspect called Jenkin and he was at the time waiting for the start of a trial for the murder of another girl. But the police also made it clear that there were other relevant facts, such as the closeness of the Seaman's Mission to Linda's home, suggesting

Constable Ovens. Laura Carter

that the accused may well have seen his victim there and then followed her to the woods.

The information from forensic experts clouded all the issues. No blood or other evidence relating to Scott's nearness to Linda was found on her body; only her own blood was on her person. There was no single article at all on the accused or from him, indicating contact with the child. When asked if he killed Linda, Scott then said that he did not. So what was the court to make of Inspector Lake's statement about Scott writing a confession? Scott started to meander from one statement to another, seeming to say that he had only been with the dead girl for ten minutes that day and then at other times contradicting this.

Durand, on the attack again as things escalated and became complex, challenged Scott's allegation that the police had threatened to take him to a cell and beat him up. A string of witnesses now came forward, mostly confirming that Scott had indeed been at the Seaman's Mission earlier that afternoon. Scott's landlady in Mangle Street made a telling statement – that he had come back to his room at twenty to five that day and that he did not look ruffled or disturbed. She washed his shirts, she said, and had there been any blood on his garments, she would have seen the stains.

In court, it reached the point at which there was a possibility of the charge being manslaughter. Everything depended on whether it was believed that the confession had been forced from Scott. The defence lawyer said: 'If you accept that Linda died by asphyxia caused by lying in her own vomit . . . then you accept that there is no evidence that whoever killed this girl either inflicted on her such bodily harm or was utterly reckless as to whether he killed her or not, and he is therefore not guilty of murder but manslaughter . . .'

But Durand saw the case as a clear case of murder. He was sure that Scott had invented the tale of being threatened and forced to sign a confession. The judge, careful to give only the facts, cast doubts on the various alibis, and also suggested that there was a need to be very careful in evaluating any evidence from children. After more than an hour, the jury returned a murder verdict. Scott was sentenced to life imprisonment but maintained his innocence up to the day of his death.

The real complication of this case becomes evident when we consider another. Two months before Linda's death, there had been another murder of a young girl and Jenkin was the man charged. The victim was Janice Holmes, twelve years old and from the village of Binbrook, twelve miles away. Janice and a friend, in April 1959, went for a walk and the latter left her to walk home alone. It was the last time that Janice was seen alive. She did not arrive home and, as the alarm was raised, a search began. Janice was found raped and dead just 400 yards from her home, at two in the morning. Could her killer also be the real killer of Linda?

It was a small, tightly-knit community and the police soon questioned everyone. Looks turned to the newest person to arrive at Binbrook, a man called Jenkin, who had supposedly gone out on his bike to fetch some lemonade but had been out alone for a long time that evening. Then a tobacco tin was found in the straw near to where the girl's body was found. It looked as though the police had a major suspect. Jenkin did have very minor cuts and scratches, but there was nothing conclusive with regard to any struggle on the part of

Linda Brown. Laura Carter

Janice Holmes. Laura Carter

his supposed victim. He had been rounded on by one local and asked what he had done with Janice, to which he replied: 'There are other folk in this village besides me.'

But there was enough circumstantial evidence to charge Jenkin so he appeared in court and faced a gruelling interview as well. The press had been so interested in the case that there had to be a discussion on the matter of a possible pre-trial. To avoid prejudice on the part of the newspapers the public were sent out of the court. But it was decided that there was a case to answer, and Jenkin went to Nottingham Assizes to stand trial for murder.

In Nottingham, Jenkin pleaded not guilty and a supposed prison confession was dismissed. The main bone of contention was the presence of Jenkin's tobacco tin at the scene of the murder. Nothing emerged at the trial and a re-trial was ordered, this time in Birmingham. What happened was that the witness from Lincoln prison told the court the tale of the confession. He said that Jenkin had told him how he had got hold of Janice, shaken her and left her motionless. The defence lawyer cross-examined Jenkin and there was doubt cast, although he gave a good reason for retelling the confession, in that his own daughter visited him and he thought of the parents of the dead girl in a different way. But matters became problematical when Jenkin told his own story. He said that Mrs Holmes had been hysterical as she challenged him and demanded to know what he had done with Janice. When asked why he had not simply gone to get the lemonade he rather whimsically said: 'You look a bit silly asking for lemonade in a pub.'

Basically, as defence counsel pointed out, all that was put against Jenkin was the tobacco tin being on the spot and the fact that a drug-user and convict had alleged that the man had made a confession behind bars. It must have seemed that there was little against the man, particularly as his wife had noticed that he was clean, even down to his shoes, when he came home that night from his bike-ride. It was also pointed out that Janice was a 'clean-living girl' who would not have gone with a man to any rendezvous. But on the other hand, as the prosecution countered, the 'gaolbird' and drug-user had told the same story to three separate people and the tobacco tin's presence could not be explained.

After over two hours of deliberation, the jury found Jenkin guilty of murder and he subsequently served sixteen years. He had a record of small crimes since his youth. In contrast, Scott served forty-four years in gaol, dying in prison in 2003. All kinds of factors in the two cases made sense at the time, but others have remained mysteries to this day.

# CHAPTER 35

# A Sad Case
# 1959

## Some stories of killings reach the high tragedy of Shakespeare . . .

Sometimes, a mere 'crime story' reaches the heights of real tragedy. The pain involved is inexplicable and the human torment lives on. The act of merely trying to recreate the series of events around these tales is painful. Such was the story of a strangling in Grimsby – something done not by a stranger in the night or a desperate and deranged psychopath, but within the family – the saddest scenario of them all.

In May 1959 a man's body was found drowned at the Royal Dock. He was James Flegg, aged forty-nine, of Nunsthorpe and the police had been looking for him for a few weeks. They wanted to talk to him because his wife, Ethel Winifred, had been found dead in their home, her body lying on the settee when she was found by a neighbour. Winifred, as Mrs Flegg was generally known, had been strangled. The tale is all the more woeful when it is recorded that the couple had five children.

Dr David Price, a Home Office pathologist, examined Winifred's body and from that point it was a case of homicide and most certainly murder. It was murder, for sure, and it was the third Monday murder in Grimsby over a three-week period, after the children previously described in the other cases of this *annus horribilis* for Grimsby.

The story began to unfold when two children, Doreen and Michael, went to knock on the door of a neighbour's house. They asked the neighbours if they could 'Come and waken mummy, as she's asleep and won't wake up!' The lady who opened the door to the children was Gladys Darnell, and she was the person who found Mrs Flegg's body, on the settee. It was school time in the

# Mother of 5 found dead at home

## POLICE ANXIOUS TO INTERVIEW HER HUSBAND

*From our Grimsby correspondent*

AFTER two children had knocked on the door of a neighbour's house and asked the occupant "to come and waken mummy, who was asleep and would not wake up," Mrs. Ethel Winifred Flegg, a 39-year-old mother of five, was found dead yesterday at her home in Milton Road, Nunsthorpe, Grimsby.

The neighbour, 29-year-old Mrs. Gladys Darnell, found Mrs. Flegg lying on a settee in the living room. The Deputy Chief Constable of Grimsby, Superintendent J. A. Skinner, said later, " We are anxious to interview the husband of the dead woman, James Flegg, who may be able to assist us in our inquiries."

Mr. Flegg was described as being aged 49, 5ft. 9in. in height, slim or medium build, and having brown hair parted on the left side. He has two warts on his right cheek and a war wound scar on his right shoulder blade. He is believed to be wearing a new brown suit with red flecks, brown shoes, a light coloured pullover, maroon tie and a fawn belted double-breasted raincoat.

Mrs. Flegg's five children are aged from eight to 19 years. It was Doreen (14) and Michael (9) who made the visit to Mrs. Darnell's house which led to the discovery.

A Home Office pathologist, Dr. David Price, travelled from Barnsley to Grimsby and in the evening

**Mr. James Flegg**     **Mrs. Flegg**

carried out a post-mortem examination. He was accompanied by Mr. J. L. Fish, of the Forensic Science Laboratory at Nottingham.

Mrs. Flegg and her husband, who have lived at Nunsthorpe for several years, were described by neighbours as " a quiet and pleasant couple." Mr. Flegg was formerly employed in tugs at Immingham Docks and Grimsby but recently transferred to the Marine Department of the British Transport Commission.

Headline on the Flegg murder. *Yorkshire Post*

morning when the children roused the neighbours, as the eldest child had found the body at 8.30.

From the point at which the police were on the scene, they wanted to talk to Mr Flegg, naturally. Superintendent Skinner, who was Deputy Chief Constable of Grimsby at the time, put together a description of James Flegg for circulation: he was forty-nine, five feet nine inches tall, with brown hair parted on the left side. He was a man with some distinctive features: two warts on one cheek and a scar (a war wound) across his right shoulder blade. He also had a scar on one earlobe. There was good reason to believe that the last time he was seen he was wearing a new brown suit with red flecks in the pattern, with a

light-coloured pullover and a maroon tie. His overcoat was fawn,
double-breasted and with a belt.

James Flegg worked in the marine section of British Transport,
based at Grimsby Docks. Previously, he worked as a tug
watchman at both Grimsby and Immingham. People who knew
the Fleggs said that they were a 'happy couple' and that Mrs
Flegg was the mother of an 'ideal family'. Only a few days before
this tragedy the pair were seen going out together and they were
noted to be heard chatting.

As the search for James Flegg began, a Home Office pathologist, Dr David Price, came to Grimsby to carry out a
post-mortem examination, accompanied by J L Fish of the
Forensic Science Laboratory, Nottingham.

The hunt for James Flegg went into full swing. Ships and
warehouses around the docks were searched. He had last been
seen on the fish docks at around five in the morning, three hours
before his wife's body was found. One report said that he had
been noticeably willing to discuss his family matters with workmates. It seemed that he may have gone further than the docks,
though, as his red cycle was missing from home. But the obvious
first move would have been to drag the docks area. That would
have been a huge task, as DCI Wagstaff of Grimsby CID told the
press at the time. Afterwards, enquiries escalated.

Scotland Yard came on the scene and transmitted radio signals
to the North Sea trawler fleet. The message to skippers was:
'Check your crew. If you have an Englishman called Flegg
aboard, detain him.' This happened because one local source
told the police that a man who appeared to answer the description of Flegg signed on for work at dawn on the day following the
killing, to work on a small fishing vessel – according to some, a
Danish ship. The search for the man across the North Sea was
the widest sea radio search for a man since that for the infamous
Dr Crippen in 1910. The Danish ship turned out to be the forty-
ton *Ella*, but when Danish police were waiting for her to dock in
Esbjerg, the news was negative: 'Sorry, only Danes aboard.'

But the search was thorough and persistent and no one was
taking anything for granted. The report was that Danish police
still intended to board her and search, at the very least to find out
if the captain had perhaps been approached by Flegg back home
in Grimsby. But all this was for nothing. Flegg's body was found
and identified by his eldest son, Barry, and the inquest was held
on the 25 May, then adjourned for fourteen days. The story has
to go down in the chronicles of Grimsby as a sad tale – one of the

saddest ever told. In a case such as this one, writers and historians cannot avoid looking at the repercussions and feeling that some communities never recover and perhaps never forget the pain that lives on. The business was, on the positive side, a feather in the cap for the police and indeed for Scotland Yard since both proved to be able to do the right things. The police's task in finding James Flegg must have seemed hopeless, but at least they had a plan of campaign.

# CHAPTER 36

# The Pirate Trawlermen 1966

## Five men were put in fear of their lives

This is a tale of pirates, but it happened nowhere near the Caribbean and the villains had no eye-patches or parrots on their shoulders. In fact, they instilled fear and panic into a ship's crew – and it happened near Grimsby.

In early July 1966, five trawlermen put into action a plot they had been hatching for some time: to take over the trawler *Loveden* in the North Sea. By 15 July they were in court facing a charge of piracy on the high seas, a charge that seems almost Elizabethan or at least from the world of movies and television dramas, but it happened, and not far off Grimsby. In the magistrates' court, James Angus, Chief Constable of Grimsby, told the tale of how the men had put together the plot, and then took over the ship. They had bound the skipper and cook hand and foot before stopping the vessel and loading a lifeboat with supplies. An epic rowing trip to Germany began.

But the skipper broke free and broadcast a mayday call on the radio. The pirates were taken in by a German ship and transported to Emden. Ernest Durrant and his crew were put in fear of their lives. The men also stole a large amount of goods, including nearly 200 bottles of beer, over 2,000 cigarettes and almost six pounds of tobacco.

The exploit was no fun for skipper Durrant and his loyal men though as they were locked in cabins all Saturday night and most of the Sunday before the skipper broke free. Even as he made the call, Durrant was attacked by the rebels and he was later forced back into his 'prison'.

Christopher Bourke, prosecuting, recalled how Durrant was tuning his wireless when he was overcome by the thugs. Of course, as they made their move to set off for Germany, they also stole the lifeboat. If it were not for the terrifying ordeal of the men overhauled by the pirates, it might be a tale with a humorous edge, as Bourke hinted when he said: 'Happily, in modern times the charge of piracy does not overcrowd the assize lists but there are crimes from time to time on the high seas in which there are elements of violence, confinement, fear instilled in the victims and theft.' He noted that there were other well-known rudiments of piracy involved in this case, and that indeed there was no other term for the offence other than piracy.

Piracy is defined in international law and governed by the Nations Convention on the Law of the Sea as 'any illegal acts of violence or detention, or any act of depredation, committed for private ends by the crew or the passengers of a private ship or aircraft and directed . . . on high seas . . . against persons or property on board said ship . . .' Everything in that definition was committed by Rodney Sherriff and his gang.

The *Loveden* sailed from Grimsby on Saturday 9 July, heading for the North Sea fishing grounds with a crew of ten men. The five pirates were noticed drinking freely, having beer and wine. The alcohol was giving them Dutch courage, no doubt, as they had devilment in mind and they had thought through what they would actually do to get the boat and the booze and set off on their mad adventure. A beer ration was usual practice on trawlers but the five men's state was extremely intoxicated by late afternoon. It was around five in the evening – when Durrant was in the wireless room – that the attack began. One of the attackers, Alwin Call, came into that room and asked for a message to be sent to his mother. As the skipper tuned to the Humber radio, Call and a man called Gibson set about him, then fastened him secure and put him on a bunk. The cook, asked to go to the skipper's cabin, was grabbed and treated in the same way. This cook, named Pepper, was a tough and determined character who went on fighting to set himself free and the skipper tried to send a distress signal. After that it became quite brutal, as the two men were tied at the neck and, as the prosecution described it, 'Were led like cattle to the forehold where the trawler nets are stored and were confined there in the darkness for the next few hours.'

The mate was then taken and locked in his cabin, before the desperadoes lowered the lifeboat and rowed for shore. They were rounded up at various places and detained. They ended up at the Buckingham Assizes at Aylesbury in October and it was there that they were found guilty of commiting an act of piracy. One of the five accused had his not guilty plea accepted. The men had taken possession of ship, committed serious assaults, and had stolen on a very large scale.

The end of the adventure was rather pathetic, however. The pirates were fooled into thinking that they were being helped, but in fact they were taken and extradited. It was alleged that Call was the ringleader and he was given one three-year and one five-year sentence to run concurrently. The others were given shorter periods of custody.

Had the men been serving in the armed forces, the piracy charge carried the punishment of death until the Crime and Disorder Act of 1998. That would have applied because they had committed 'piracy with violence'. We have to wonder whether or not these rogues studied the statute law and guidelines on capital punishment before their escapade. But all talk of adventure and derring-do put aside, the bottom line is that this gang terrorised five men on those horrendous two days of drink-fused violence and mayhem. It was easy for some of the press at the time to make this seem like a drunken plan of the hare-brained variety. From one viewpoint it was, but from the point of view of common sense and order, it was horrific.

# CHAPTER 37

# Why Was He Set Free?
# 1967

## He embarked on a prolonged violent and ferocious attack with a knife . . .

Sometimes, to quote from Shakespeare, 'The law is an ass.' At other times the system looks as though it is made to allow gross and terrible mistakes. In the area of mental health, this is a recurrent problem. We seem to read all the time about 'escaped lunatics' as they were called at one time. This is a case in that category, and it cries out for reason to have been applied. Unfortunately, it was not.

When a mental patient was allowed to discharge himself from hospital, it seems that no one thought he would be a particular problem. But how wrong that line of thought was can be seen in the tragic consequences of his release. Ivy Sharpe, sixty-five years old, was murdered on 18 July 1967.

Leonard Harding, of Cleethorpes, embarked on a prolonged violent and ferocious attack on Ivy Sharpe. What developed was a classic example of one of those homicide cases in which, however lamentable the consequences for the victim and victim's family, there is an issue of mental instability on the part of the attacker. So the court deliberated on this murder at Lincoln Assizes before Mr Justice O'Connor.

It was a case of Harding being able to offer a plea of manslaughter, as his personality defects opened up the possibility of his being considered an instance of diminished responsibility. The prosecution lawyer, Michael Davies, explained that Harding had a long-standing mental illness and had received treatment at Rampton Hospital. At the time, the word 'Rampton' signified all kinds of cultural importance, as the media had made the place into something fearful, suggesting Victorian austerity and severely dangerous inmates. But Harding had in fact been transferred to Worcester and, after his stay there, was considered an

# JUDGE ASKS WHY MAN WAS FREED

Mr. Justice O'Connor asked at Lincolnshire Assizes at Lincoln yesterday why a mental patient was allowed to discharge himself from hospital two months before he stabbed a widow to death.

Leonard John Harding, aged 25, bakery machinist, of Neville Street, Cleethorpes, was charged with the murder of Mrs. Ivy May Sharpe, aged 65, at Grimsby on July 18. His plea of manslaughter on the grounds of diminished responsibility was accepted and an order was made committing him to Rampton Hospital indefinitely.

Mr. Michael Davies, for the prosecution, said that Mr. Harding had suffered from mental illness for some time and had been treated at Rampton Hospital. He was transferred to another hospital at Worcester earlier this year and was treated as an informal patient and allowed to discharge himself.

Two months later, he went to see Mrs. Sharpe, a tailoress. Because of some words they had, he "embarked on a prolonged violent and ferocious attack with a knife", from which Mrs. Sharpe died.

Dr. Maurice Fowles, medical officer of Lincoln Prison, said Mr. Harding was suffering from psychiatric disorder.

The judge asked him if he knew why the man, "obviously a terrible danger", was set free. Dr. Fowles said he understood that authorities at Rampton felt he had improved sufficiently to be transferred from strict supervision to another hospital.

Making the order committing Mr. Harding to Rampton indefinitely, the judge told him: "You are a dangerous man who requires strict medical supervision for as long as may be thought necessary."

'Judge Asks Why Man Was Freed'. *The Times*

'informal' patient. That term implies that someone thought him to be clear of any psychopathic tendencies or dangerous schizophrenic features in his mental profile.

When Harding paid a visit to Mrs Sharpe, who was a tailoress, he let loose the savagery in his tempestuous nature. The medical officer at Lincoln prison could only say that the attacker was suffering from 'a mental disorder' and that was a familiar scenario in courts across the land at that time. A regular non-specialist doctor was asked to pass an opinion in court on a person who may have been suffering from any one of a number of extreme bi-polar states or schizophrenia. But of course, within the limits of psychiatric knowledge then, it is partly understandable that Dr Fowles (from the prison) said – after being asked why Harding had been released – 'He was thought to have improved sufficiently to be transferred from strict supervision to another hospital.'

It was back to Rampton for the killer. The judge made an order for the man's committal there with the words: 'You are a dangerous man who requires strict medical supervision for as long as may be thought necessary.' It was an indefinite committal order. With the wisdom of hindsight, we can see that now we live in an age of medical specialists, and the subject of Forensic Psychology has become a university course. The television series *Cracker* has made everyone aware of the complexities of illnesses such as schizophrenia and bi-polar conditions. In simpler times, that was not the case and there were too many tough questions asked of general physicians about cases like that of Harding.

# CHAPTER 38

# Some Curiosities Not So Foul

G rimsby and the surrounding area have seen some crimes that have a strong relationship to the industry and the pattern of settlement and development of North East Lincolnshire. The position on the Humber estuary has meant that many crimes have been nautical, and often confined to internal enquiry. The inquiries held at the Grimsby Exchange often have some of the most exciting and intriguing cases, though they are often not so much crimes as misdemeanours – human error is the focus. Often, these records involve as much heroism as folly. A typical example is the story of the *Belldock,* a trawler stranded on the Balta Sound in 1954.

After the inquiry, the skipper was removed by the Ministry of Transport, so there was a degree of seriousness in this tale. The skipper and the mate had struggled for control of the ship on the rocks and she eventually violently ran aground. The cause of the fight and ensuing disaster was put down to excessive drinking and there were questions asked about the large amount of drink stored on board the trawlers at the time. The core of the disaster was that an experienced seaman, George Brown, had gone to the bridge and tried to teach the captain and mate (neither knew the Balta Sound) how to cope in the developing gale. Brown testified, however, that the two men had drunk a great deal of rum and had also been playing around with the vessel's telegraph system. Brown's experience counted for nothing against that behaviour. Luckily, there was no loss of life. The events had happened in a wild and vulnerable place and the excess of drink had turned what could have been a manageable situation into near disaster and loss of life. The man with the good sense and experience had not been listened to and drink-related insanity took over.

There have been other stories, some great and some tragic, though on a minor scale. What follows are some of the lost and interesting tales that never quite made it into the mainstream records of Grimsby crime.

## Crazy Libel

Not all of the cases from Grimsby and Cleethorpes that ended up in the courts were so nasty, extreme or dramatic as pirate attacks and killings. Take for instance the libel case in 1925 when a fisherman of Grimsby had his marriage planned, to a lady who was a celebrated local singer. Clearly, that event was of great interest to the local press. So much was this the case that the newspaper printed a full account of the wedding ceremony – but the day before by mistake. The report read: 'The honeymoon is being spent in the South of England.' Of course, as soon as the man in question arrived for work at the fish market, he was a figure of fun. The line of attack was something like: 'You soon got tired of the lady!'

This led to an action for libel against the *Grimsby Times and Telegraph*. Unfortunately, it meant no satisfaction for the victim, as the ruling was that the action was 'frivolous and vexatious'. We have to feel some sympathy for him, but the law had no redress, and his torment at the hands of his workmates went on and on. Luckily for the newspaper staff, the culprit was never found. If he was, the story of what was said and done has not come down to us.

## A Sad Suicide

There are also other cases which might have been included, such as the unremitting catalogue of lamentable suicides – an act which was a crime in England until 1961. What those tales do tell us today is how the community coped with such terrible deeds as time went on and a more profound understanding of depression was developed. A typical case is that of Alice Collins, in 1937. She was found gassed in her own home, and had previously tried to drown herself. An act of heroism by Leading Aircraftman William Constable, who brought her out of the River Freshney on that first attempt, was all for nothing. The court heard that all-too-familiar phrase: 'Suicide while of unsound mind' spoken by the magistrate. Every time a suicide is described and retold in crime case books, the tough reminder that suicide was a crime until 1961 has to be said: a fact very hard to believe today, with our more enlightened views on such topics as depression and mental illness.

## The RSPCA

There have also been many stories of 'foul deeds' that have been despicable and unsavoury, giving offence to any right-thinking person. Under that category we have to look at cruelty to animals, and in the 1890s there were several such cases. One notably unpleasant example is that of Harry Kominsky, who was a Doncaster horse-dealer. He appeared in the Grimsby Police Court in 1894 after RSPCA inspectors investigated his trade in horses. He walked his animals from Doncaster to Grimsby with the aim of having them shipped to Antwerp. Five of his sixteen animals were found to be in a pitiful state. The inspector reported that 'The animals were suffering from various painful diseases which rendered a journey of nearly sixty miles a positive torture to them.' The report on Kominsky pointed out that he gave them neither food nor water except what they could get by the road, on that long journey.

The poor creatures suffered again when on board ship. Kominsky tried to claim that they were quite fit for the journey but his argument failed to impress, and he was fined six guineas. He was not the owner, however, simply the manager. His employers were also fined heavily. Everyone involved in that despicable case has to take some blame, of course. Anyone in the line of staff involved could have stopped the cruelty.

## Teenage Skipper Steals a Ship

Small tales of the sea and hare-brained schemes out of harbour also fill the Grimsby crime records. There are hundreds of interesting events, but few so bizarre as that of the teenager in 1959 who stole a ship, all alone, and took it out to sea. He stole the ship and diesel oil and brought it back. Lawyer J G Howarth told the court: 'There is no other case in which a young man (he was only eighteen) has taken a fishing vessel out to sea and brought her back safely . . .' So proud of his mariner's skills was the young man that he was irritated by the fact that a tug came out to meet him, when he was sure he could have brought the ship, *Ann's*, back on his own. He had wanted to prove to himself and others that he could do such a thing alone, and only a strong wind had prevented him.

This was certainly not new. In 1893, two young men took over a tug, had a 'joy ride' and struck out of harbour by telling the gateman that they were simply going round to the other dock. They were seen by the Killingholme coastguard, and one of the boys' fathers had sailed past them on another ship during the course of their escapade. The coastguard boarded the ship (the *Star*) and all was sorted out. There is no record of what followed from father to son, but we can guess.

## Drug-running

Also at sea, modern smuggling has its own chronicle. In 1922, drugs were still making the headlines, as in the case of David Davis, a bootmaker who fancied making some easy money. He stashed a massive amount of cocaine in a German steamer but was too amateur in that trade and the stash was discovered. For hiding 100 bottles of cocaine worth £3,000 he was given no clemency and headed for gaol.

### £3,000 WORTH OF COCAINE.

#### SMUGGLING CHARGE AT GRIMSBY.

Following the seizure by Customs officials at Grimsby of a large quantity of cocaine, found in a passenger's trunk in a steamer from Germany, as reported in *The Times* yesterday, proceedings were begun in the Grimsby Police Court yesterday.

David Davis, aged fifty-seven, described as a bootmaker, was charged with importing and concealing one hundred bottles of cocaine, valued at £3,000. The defendant, who is an Australian, looked ill, and was legally represented.

Chief Preventive Officer Forth stated that the accused arrived on board the steamship Accrington with the cocaine in his possession. He asked for a remand of seven days because of the seriousness of the offence. This was granted. Mr. Collinson, for the prisoner, asked for bail on the grounds of ill-health, but the Magistrate, in the absence of medical evidence, refused the application.

Cocaine smuggling case, 1922. *The Times*

## The Grimsby Fagin

The Grimsby 'Fagin' also has a minor role in the criminal history of the town. In 1927, Herbert Reade, reported in the papers as 'A coloured man with wicked criminality' ran a gang of child thieves around the docks. This came out after two teenagers had been arrested for stealing a haul of groceries from ships in the harbour. When the boys had been told to steal, they complained that they had no idea how to pick locks, so 'Fagin' Reade showed them how and set them to work. Police found the stash of stolen foods in Reade's house. It was rightly said that in doing this he had corrupted the lads and 'set them on a career of crime'. He had originally been given six months' imprisonment but at the court of appeal everything went haywire for the crook, and his sentence was actually increased to eighteen months.

## Vicious Teamwork, 1868

An incident which illustrates the necessity for teamwork in crooks comes from 1868, when William Proctor took a lift on a cart going from Cleethorpes to Grimsby. There were two women in the cart and on the journey, one put her arms around him and the other one started beating him with an umbrella. They were 'on the game' and it was an event that brought about more hilarity than sympathy. In court people were amused by the mishap and assault. Someone said: 'One of the prisoners seemed to fall in love with the prosecution.'

## Crimes Swept Under the Carpet

All that is left of Upper Burgess Street today - centre of the kind of street crime described. The author

Where does the historian stand on investigating 'crimes of in-decency?' In the Victorian period these things were reported minimally, as in the case of fisherman William Cordiner, who was accused of 'ill-using' two boys while on board a fishing smack. This was quite a rare crime, and he was found guilty. Cordiner was only eighteen, and was found guilty of gross inde-cency and given two years' hard labour. It was the category of crime which was always destined for the small print and the embarrassed use of vague terms and euphemisms in Victorian crime reporting. Almost certainly, it was more common than written accounts would suggest.

## A Guilty Plea before the Trial

A hundred years ago a petty thief accused of stealing some clothes in Grimsby, when faced with the long arm of the law, said: 'Shall I be tried on Tuesday? If so, I shall plead guilty and get it finished.' It was a seemingly stupid and rash statement that was to lead the man to the Court of Appeal. Edward Hewson was tried at Lincoln Assizes and given a sentence of three years of penal servitude. The evidence consisted of two details: first he had identified the stolen clothes and second, a pawnbroker stated that Hewson brought the said clothes to be pledged at his shop.

At appeal, Hewson's lawyer claimed that the circumstances of his man being identified by the pawnbroker were unacceptable as good evidence. Hewson had said the words about pleading guilty to a police officer while chatting, and that coloured the view of the listening pawnbroker, the lawyer sensibly argued. But then Hewson had not called witnesses to speak for him, choosing to write down what they had said, to read out in court. Isaac Knighton, the bootmaker to whom Hewson had gone that day to have a boot mended, was called to provide an alibi. Unfortunately for Hewson, both Knighton and his young lady assistant could not specify a day or a time at which the crook might have called.

In explaining his decision to quash the appeal, the Lord Chief Justice was harsh on poor Miss Dean, the shop assistant, saying: 'Miss Dean was totally useless as she could not remember the day on which she saw the prisoner at all!' Tact was not His Lordship's strong point.

## A Naughty Nineties Fraud in Cleethorpes

Edward Frayne was a collector for the Royal London Insurance Company. The system then was that collectors in the provinces took a cut from the profits gained when new customers were signed up to policies. Frayne fell into the easy temptation (common in many areas) of making life less complicated and demanding by inventing clients. He was found out and given three months' hard labour. That kind of new fraud was always happening, and the insurance companies had to adapt and learn from such straightforward ways of being subject to scams. Throughout the nineteenth century, the insurance companies were 'finding their feet' in terms of how to cope with their clients and also their regional staff. A learning experience for them was usually costly, as with Mr Frayne.

## Arch Villain from Grimsby?

According to some conspiracy theorists, the greatest and most high profile of all Grimsby villains was Albert Alexander Osborne. Some historians of the Kennedy assassination place this chubby son of a Grimsby businessman on the scene. There are tales of Albert training assassins and travelling across the USA and Canada, up to no good. In one study he is alleged to have been the minder and maybe even the trainer of a band of killers in Mexico, and that he travelled on the same bus as Lee Harvey Oswald, in September 1963, just a few months before the Kennedy assassination at Dallas. It seems incredible that this man could have been 'in Dallas on November 22 in charge of a team of shooters' but if he was, then no other character in these pages can match his story, and Grimsby has a new claim to fame – or infamy. Check out the bibliography if you want to know more.

## Regional Crime Stories: the Borderline Subjects

As with all crime case books on Britain, Grimsby and Cleethorpes accounts of transgressions, mistakes and downright evil deeds always leave a few gaps. There are questions historians in this context always want to ask. It was not possible, for instance, to follow up reactions and responses to the McGill postcards case; clearly there was fear and apprehension around at the time and businesses were severely affected. No one likes the idea of a police raid on the high street. Then there are the marginal cases purposely left out such as plaintive suicides with little need to add a detailed story to the bare fact of a person taking his or her own life; also some stories fade out in the records so that we have no knowledge of how a particular perpetrator of a crime ends up in life (or death). The most common cul-de-sac in that respect is the story of a mental patient, as in the workhouse murder of Mrs Robinson (Chapter 21). But I hope that this survey has at least cast some light on a rather alternative view of the criminal history of the area.

## The Conflicts

At the heart of these stories has been the various dissensions familiar in British society through the ages: rich and poor, haves and have-nots and so on, but the 1950s stand out. The immediate postwar years, after the state and people were exhausted following the struggle with Hitler, were years of austerity. Rationing did not end until 1954 and many families were on the poverty line. Grimsby was particularly badly hit at that time and there was a severe and widespread knock-on effect on urban crime in the region. The decade became the time in which the notion of the murderer attacking at random, armed robbery with ex-service guns and attacks on the elderly and vulnerable, all increased. Many of the smaller scale crime stories fall into that category – stories of minor attacks and fights, police assaults and so on. Under the main crime stories, there was always another

Sir Rufus Isaacs – a busy man on several of these cases. Andy Tennick

current flowing, pointing out the way in which the Grimsby area mirrored national crime. All ports were notably open to scams and frauds of all kinds in those years of shortages, when employees often ripped off employers and the ledgers never really balanced in legitimate ways. But they are tales for another volume.

As a general trend, Victorian crime shifted more towards white collar offences from around the 1860s, rather than a predominance of crimes against the person, but it has always been the murders and robberies that make the headlines.

# Bibliography and Sources

## Author's note

There are a great many sources for local crime available from a multiplicity of places. In Grimsby much has been done on particular areas, notably police records. The records of police administrators have provided details on a minute scale with summary offences in close focus. Accessing the major crime had meant a reliance on a range of newspaper sources and on written records which are often hard to find. Where I have not been able to trace authors in references (in anonymous publications) I have had to paraphrase their opinions and memories. For help with all those enquiries, I owe deep thanks to the staff at Grimsby Central Library and *Scunthorpe Evening Telegraph*.

I have not had to go to the extremes of using court records or calendars of prisoners, as there has been much available already in secondary sources.

In trying to locate Bert Fryer, author of *Recollections of a Country Copper*, I have had no success, and so I owe a debt to him for rare insights into police work in the 1930s, expressed in a form almost completely unavailable elsewhere. Without that kind of memoir, all kinds of everyday insights into crime would not be available to historians. Fryer somehow found time to do more than merely take notes in his pocket book.

## Books

Geoffrey Best, *Mid-Victorian Britain 1851–75*, Fontana, 1988
James Bland, *The Common Hangman*, Zeon Books, 2001
Thomas Boghardt, *Spies of the Kaiser*, Palgrave, 2004
Frank L Bunn, *No Silver Spoon*, J Brock, 1960
David Canter, *Criminal Shadows*, Harper Collins, 1995
*Criminal Appeal Records*, Sweet and Maxwell (annual)
Oliver Cyriax, *The Penguin Encyclopaedia of Crime*, Penguin, 1996
Shani D'Cruse *et alia*, *Murder*, Willan Publishing, 2006

Joseph Dean, *Hatred, Ridicule and Contempt: a book of libel cases*, Pan, 1955

Lord Denning, *Landmarks in the Law*, Butterworths, 1984

John J Eddlestone, *The Encyclopaedia of Executions*, John Blake, 2002

Stewart P Evans, *Executioner: The Chronicles of James Berry, Victorian Hangman*, Sutton, 2004

Yvonne Ffrench and Sir John Squire, *News from the Past 1805–1887: The Autobiography of the Nineteenth Century*, Gollancz, 1960

Bert Fryer, *Recollections of a Country Copper 1936–1966*, self-published, 1966

Edward Gillett, *A History of Grimsby*, Oxford University Press, 1960

Adrian Gray, *Crime and Criminals in Victorian Lincolnshire*, Paul Watkins, 1993

Patrick Hastings, *Autobiography*, Heinemann, 1948

James Hayward, *Myths and Legends of the First World War*, Sutton, 2002

Percy Hoskins, *No Hiding Place: The full authentic story of Scotland Yard in action*, Daily Express, 1955

*Household Narrative*, Chapman and Hall, 1850

Travers Humphries, *A Book of Trials: personal recollections of an eminent Judge of the High Court*, Pan, 1956

Rufus Isaacs, *Rufus Isaacs, The First Marquis of Reading*, Hutchinson, 1942

Brian Lane, *The Encyclopaedia of Forensic Science*, Headline, 1992

Roy Porter, *Madness. A Brief History*, Oxford, 2002

Vincent Powell, *The Legal Companion*, Robson Books, 2005

Jasper Ridley, *A Brief History of The Tudor Age*, Robinson, 1998

R F Roberts, *Trawlers of Humberside*, Tempus, 2005

Robert Harborough Sherard, *The Child Slaves of Britain*, Hurst and Blackett, 1905

Jack Slipper, *Slipper of the Yard*, Sidgewick and Jackson, 1981

Martin Stallion and David S Wall, *The British Police: Police Forces and Chief Officers 1829–2000*, Police History Society, 1999

Donald Thomas, *Villains' P aradise: Britain's underworld from the spiv to the Krays*, John Murray, 2005

Geoff Tibballs, *The Murder Guide to Great Britain*, Boxtree, 1994

Chief Superintendent W Trigg, *Lincolnshire Constabulary Instruction Book*, Hedley Slack, 1920

Dinah Tyszka et alia, *Law, People and Landscapes*, Lincolnshire Books, 1991

Katherine Watson, *Poisoned Lives: English Poisoners and their Victims*, Hambledon, 2004

Ben Whitaker, *The Police*, Penguin, 1964

Mick Woodley, *Osborn's Concise Law Dictionary*, Thomson, 2005
Douglas Wynn, *The Crime Writer's Handbook*, Allison and Busby, 2003

## Newspapers and periodicals

*Annual Register*
*BBC History Magazine*
*Daily Mail*
*Grimsby Evening Telegraph*
*Grimsby News*
*History Today*
*Journal of the Police History Society*
*Journal of Social History*
*Murder Most Foul*
*Punch*
*Scunthorpe Evening Telegraph*
*The Times*
*The Times Digital Archive*
*True Crime Magazine*
*The Yorkshire Post*

## Reports and Miscellaneous

*Chief Constable's Annual Reports*, Roberts and Jackson, Grimsby, 1918
*Criminal Statistics and Annual Returns 1911*, Roberts and Jackson, 1912
Fred W Riggall, 'The Early History of Grimsby', *Grimsby Gazette*, 1920 *The Skelton Collection*, Grimsby Library

## Unpublished Dissertation

Cynthia J Stringfellow, *Sources and Methods in a Study of 19th Century Crime in Grimsby*, Humberside Polytechnic, 1991

## Web Sites

www.hobrad.com/osborne.htm
www.murderfiles.com

# Index

**People**

Abbot of Whitby  7
Allbones, Sergeant  38
Ambler, Edith May  94–5
Andrews, Stephen  10
Aske, Robert  15
Athelwold, King  4
Atkin, Lord  102

Baglee, Detective Inspector  57
Baring-Gould, Sabine  17
Bateman, Detective Sergeant  126
Bennett, Major  95
Berry, James  49
Billington, James  56
Blackbourn, Mr  132
Blundell, Mr  97
Borrell, Edward  21
Bourke, Christopher  147
Bourne, Cardinal  86
Brand, Otto  2, 62
Brandon, Charles  17
Bray, Edwin  10
Bray, Palmer  10
Brightmore, James  83–4
Brigsely, Roger de  10
Brook, Joseph  112–13
Brown, George  153
Brown, Linda  137–8
Buller, Fitzwalter  134
Bun, frank L  2
Burgess, Mr  39–40
Butterley, George  50–1
Button, Edward  3, 26–7

Call, Alwin  148
Carter, Jean  99
Catherall, Barbara  16
Chance, William  87
Chapman, John  34
Collins, Alice  154
Constable, William  154
Cordiner, William  158
Cornwall, Earl of  4
Crawford, Mr  41–2

Cross, Mr  102
Curtis, Anthony  17

Daubney, Joseph  20, 25
Davies, Michael  143
Davis, David  156
De Boer,  82
Defoe, Daniel  1
Dickinson, Edward  3
Dines, Mrs  26
Durand, Victor  138
Durrant, Ernest  147–8

Edwards, Arthur  91–2
Edwards, Reginald  81–2

Faulding, Richard  23
Field, Mr Justice  45
Flegg, James  143–5
Flegg, Winifred  143–5
Fowler, William  126–8
Folwes, Dr  151
Francis, Inspector  91
Frayne, Edward  158–9
Frow, Henry  130–32
Fry, Sir Edward  74
Fryer, Bert  2, 100, 107–10

Ganth  8
Gilbert and Sullivan  35
Gillett, Edward  64
Gloody, James  58
Goddard  6
Godrich;  6
Goldborow  4
Goodison, Mr  64
Grim  3

Hall, Edward  26
Hall, William  3
Hallam, John  18
Hardcastle, Sergeant  37
Harding, Leonard  150–1
Hastings, Sir Patrick  104
Havelok  4, 6

Heneage, Edward 31
Henry III 12
Henry VIII 15
Hewson, Edward 158
Holmes, Janice 140–1
Holmes, Valentine 106
Howarth, J G 155
Humphries, Travers 100
Humphrey, Mary 115–19
Hutson, Eric 100

Insole, Richard 45–8
Insole, Sarah 45–8
Isaacs, Rufus 160

Jenkin, James 141–2
Jones, Thomas 94–5

Kell, Vernon 79
Kendall, Thomas 16
Kennedy, Mr Justice 78
Keyworth, William 21
Kominsky, Harry 155
Kyme, Guy 16–17

Larkin, Philip 1
Lascelles, Sir Frank 57
Lawrence, Commander 103
Lawrence, D H 79
Le fever, J Shaw 88
Len, William de 7
Lindes, Walter de la 13
Livingstone, David 68
Lumley, Thomas 10
Lyons, P C 127

McBean, Captain 83–4
McGill, Donald 122–25
Mallison, Ling 138
Marples, Bobby 88
Marshal, William 20, 25
Masterman, Walter 96–7
Melton, Nicholas 16
Morland, William 17
Mudd, Alderman 65
Muller, Karl 81

O'Callaghan, Bridget 115–19
Olsson, Ernst 79–81
Orsborne, Skipper 103–07

Orwell, George 121, 123
Osborne, Albert 159
Oswald, Harvey 159
Ovens, Constable 138

Papper, William 62
Pearson, Patrick 115
Peel, Sir Roberrt 2
Powell, Anthony 121
Preston, Gilbert de 12
Price, Dr David 143
Proctor, William 157
Purser, Inspector 127

Rainer, Frederick 51
Rawnsley, W F 1
Reade, Herbert 157
Robinson, Mary 86–7
Roenthal, Robert 81
Rumbold, Henry 53–5
Rushby, Harriet 53–5

Scott, Herbert 138–39
Sharpe, Ivy 150
Sherard, Roberrt 66
Sindall, Superintendent 95
Sizer, Lucy 41
Slipper, Jack 136
Smethurst, Henry 56
Smith, Brian 130–3
Smith, John 58
Smith, Lucy 76–8
Smith, Samuel 76–8
Stattersfield, David 2

Terry, Benjamin 49
Tew, Superintendent 137

Vincent, Mr 50

Waltham, William de 12
Ward, Lipson 81
Ward, Mrs. 77
Watchet, Simon de 12
Watkin, Mr 34
Waters, Edward 17
Williams, Lord Chief Justice 40
Wilson, John 2
Wintringham, Tom 3
Woodhall, Joseph 86–7

Yarborough. Lord 31
Young, Hugo 96

**Places**
Antwerp 155
Auckland Road fish docks 103
Aylesbury 149
Aylesby church 10

Balta Sound 153
Barnetby 130–1
Barry 126
Barton Police Court 91
Binbrook 140
Blyton 39–40
Bradley Haverstoe 19–22
Bradford 72
Bremen 82
Brighton 123
Brighton Road 109
Buckingham Palace 58
Burgess Street 66

Caistor 16
Caistor Poor Law Union 88
Clee 17
Cleethorpes, 38, 50–2, 83–5,
    107–110, 121–4, 137–8, 150
Cobb Hall 30

*Dolphin Hotel* 110
Doncaster 155
*Duke of York, The* 26–7

Earl Street 130
Essex 127

Federation Building 71
Fisher Lads' Institute 66
Forensic Science Laboratory 145
Fourth Terrace 76
Friskney 13

Gainsborough 39
Greetwell Road 49
Grimsby 1, 2, 3, 12, 17, 26, 38,
    61–3, 71–5, 81–4, 126–8,
    134–6
Grimsby Docks 42–4, 96–8, 145
Grimsby Magistrates' Court 115

Grimsby Police Court 50
Grimsby Road 99
Grimsby Town Hall 57

Holm manor 12
Holton-le-Clay 100
Hope Street 68, 76
Hull 3, 32, 62, 97
Humber estuary 1, 8
Humberstone 25

*Imperial Hotel* 99

Killingholme 155
King Edward Street 66

Laceby 13, 19, 21

Lincoln 6
Lincoln Assizes 118, 122, 150, 158
Lincoln Castle 10, 30
Lincoln Prison 53–4, 62
London 51
Louth 14

Manchester 83
Mangle Street 139
Milton Road, 144

Norfolk 126
Northampton 19
North Sea 147–9
Nottingham 49
Nottingham Assizes 141
Nunsthorpe 143

Portsmouth 103
Potsdam 81

Queen's Parade 95

Rampton hospital 150
Riby Square 138
River Freshney 154
Romney Marsh 7
Royal Dock 143
Rotterdam 80
*Royal Hotel, The* 34

Salisbury 19

Scarborough 17
Scartho workhouse 86–8
Scotland Yard 146
Seaman's Mission 138
Sheffield 52
Spilsby 94
Stallingborough 10
Strangeways 85
*Struggler's Inn, The* 29

Temperance Hall 73
Tiverton Street 94

Trent Navigation 1

Upper Burgess Street 157

Van Dieman's Land 43

Wakefield 39
Waltham 19
Weelsby Road 115
Weelsby Woods 137
*White Hart Inn* 40
Wootton 91–3
Worcester 95
Wrawby 132

*Yarborough Hotel* 31–33, 37